A GARDENER'S GUIDE TO

COMPOSTING
TECHNIQUES

A GARDENER'S GUIDE TO

COMPOSTING TECHNIQUES

For home, the allotment or a community garden

ROD WESTON

THE CROWOOD PRESS

CONTENTS

Introduction   6

1 Composting: History, Climate Change,
   Sites and Principles   8

2 Composting Techniques   20

3 Composting: Process and the Required
   Conditions   36

4 Phases of Hot Composting: Microorganisms,
   Macroorganisms and Pathogens   53

5 Entry-Level Composting   60

6 Mid- and Higher-Range Compost Bins   78

7 Composting for the Enthusiast and the
   Professional   93

8 Potential Problems   112

9 Compost Activators   127

10 Vermiculture: Composting with Worms   132

11 Bokashi Fermentation   145

12 Using Compost   154

13 Compost Teas and Liquid Feeds   163

   Acknowledgements   173

   Index   174

INTRODUCTION

In recent years there has been an increased interest in composting as an activity that can help to reduce greenhouse gas emissions and play a role in protecting the environment, while at the same time contributing to a healthy soil. The aim of this book is to make a small difference by encouraging householders to compost their organic waste and, most importantly, to continue composting. New composters may encounter various problems while trying to master the craft, and the drop-out rate tends to be quite high. It is hoped that detailing the different techniques and procedures to deal with any issues may help new recruits to persevere. As part of this approach, the photographs used to illustrate the text show less of the pristine bins and smart tidy gardens that often feature in books and more of the actual working bins, which can be untidy and in need of repair, and in some cases may look weedy and neglected. With a little help and knowledge, compost just happens. The composting area of a garden usually reflects the owner's general approach to gardening; appearances can vary widely, from a well-managed and professional-looking set-up to a scruffy site tucked away in a corner of the garden, hidden from view. Both approaches can be effective. The key message is to keep composting, whatever style you adopt.

Like many of my generation, as I child I helped my father on his allotment. In those days, the allotment was an important piece of ground that played a major role in providing fruit and vegetables for the family. Compost heaps, along with manure from the local stables, provided essential nutrients and organic materials for the soil. I continued composting at home and, later, on my own allotment, but it was not until I joined the National Allotment Society that I became interested in composting as more than a way of disposing of garden waste and providing a soil supplement. In 2009, I became a Garden Organic Leicestershire County Council Master Composter. My desire to promote composting and encourage both gardeners and householders to adopt it as a means of reducing waste sent to landfill led to the establishment of a demonstration site at the County Council Museum and Discovery Park in Coalville, which showed a range of home composting techniques to visitors. I then became interested in promoting small-scale community composting on allotments, community gardens and in schools, and began to give talks to allotment societies and garden clubs. Over the years, the Coalville demonstration moved venue several times until settling at its present site at Stokes Wood Allotments in Leicester. This location has a ready supply of garden waste and access to catering waste as well as indoor and outdoor training facilities. The site now provides a community composting service to allotment plot-holders and continues to demonstrate different composting bins and techniques to the public.

It was my experience as Master Composter and as a member of the NAS that led to this book. My hope is to encourage people to start composting and, once they have got going, to develop their skills and techniques, and increase the range and volume of waste that they can divert from landfill. It is also aimed at encouraging groups to set up small-scale community composting on allotments, at schools and on community gardens. If garden and catering waste can be dealt with on site, the environmental costs of transporting it to a central location for processing can be avoided.

The advice in this book is intended to be taken as a guide. All the procedures and techniques that are described can be modified to suit your own particular circumstances. There are almost as many ways of composting as there are composters and, despite what might be read online, there is no single right way of doing anything. If what you are doing works, it must be right for you, although, of course, the method may be open to improvement. The main thing is to enjoy your composting in the knowledge that, while you are improving your soil to produce better crops, you are also, in a small way, helping to save the planet.

CHAPTER 1

COMPOSTING: HISTORY, CLIMATE CHANGE, SITES AND PRINCIPLES

Composting has a long history as an effective and environmentally friendly means of waste disposal. There has been a need to dispose of animal manure and used bedding since animals were first domesticated, so it was natural that animal (and human) waste would be used as one of the main sources of soil enrichment, until the introduction of modern sewage systems, science-based farming and chemical fertilisers. Composting has developed from an activity practised by individual farmers to being the key part of the waste management and environmental systems today. This introductory chapter will look at its history, as well as advising on the basic health and safety precautions that are required when working with compost.

A Brief History of Composting

The truism that there is 'nothing new under the sun' certainly applies to composting. Many of the techniques used today have their origins in those used by early farmers. One of the first written accounts of composting dates from between 2320 and 2120 BC, when the people living in the Akkadian Empire in Mesopotamia transitioned from being hunter-gatherers to farming.

There is also evidence of small-scale cultivation in the Neolithic, Bronze Age and Iron Age in Scotland with midden heaps being ploughed into the land. By the first century BC, records show that the Chinese were enriching their soil with cooked bones, manure and silkworm debris. There are also references to the composting of manure and straw in an early Hindu text, and the Greeks, Egyptians and Romans are all known to have taken straw from animal stalls and buried it in cultivated fields. Similar practices are also mentioned in the Old Testament and the Hebrew Talmud, which records the enrichment of the soil using ashes, straw, stubble, chaff and grass, as well as the blood from animal sacrifices.

The Native Americans were active composters, using sheet and pit composting. They also composted while planting, burying uneaten fish and parts of animals as a nutrient source when sowing seeds. However, as in most areas, stable manure was more readily available than fish – evidence suggests that the early American farmers adopted a system using two loads of soil to one of farmyard manure.

Professor F.H. King of the U.S. Department of Agriculture toured China, Japan, and Korea in the early 1900s and published information on the use of manure (both animal and human), canal mud, green manure, and composts to maintain soil fertility.

Sir Albert Howard took King's writings into account when developing the Indore composting method on which many modern techniques are based. The Indore method used a mix of 3 parts plant matter to 1 part manure. These were initially piled up in sandwich fashion, with green layers of about 15cm (6in) thick followed by a 5cm (2in) layer of manure and then one of soil, ground limestone and rock phosphate. The layers were repeated until the heap was about 1.5m (5ft) high. The heap was kept moist and turned during decomposition providing aerobic conditions, and the resulting compost was ready in about three months.

Modern composting is often associated with the organic movement that began to grow in the early 1900s in response to the growth of industrial agriculture and use of synthetic chemical fertilisers and pesticides. Rudolf Steiner's system of biodynamic agriculture, developed in 1924, included the use of compost preparations involving herbs. Some of these are still used today by home composters to make liquid fertilisers and as compost activators.

In the USA, J.I. Rodale continued Howard's work and showed American gardeners the value of compost as a soil improver. In 1947 he established the Soil and Health Foundation, later to be renamed the Rodale Institute. In the UK, Lawrence D. Hills was so intrigued by the possibilities of the perennial hybrid plant Russian comfrey that he devoted much of the rest of his life to popularising its use. In 1954 Hills formed the Henry Doubleday Research Association (HDRA), which now trades as Garden Organic.

Compost: Reducing Waste

The standard definition of compost is that it is a soil conditioner produced through the aerobic biological decomposition of organic materials. Composting plays a key role in improving the structure and fertility

Compost bins at a National Trust estate. Materials are still being added to the bin on the left.

of soil and encourages microbial activity (for more on this, *see* Chapter 12). The commercial product has usually undergone decomposition at mesophilic and thermophilic temperatures (hot composting), which reduces the viability of pathogens and weed seeds. At the domestic level, while both hot- and cold-composting techniques may be used, cold composting is the more frequent choice.

Under the standard definition, anaerobic decomposition by microorganisms that do not require oxygen to survive is not composting and does not produce 'compost' but anaerobic digestate. However, many home practitioners will refer to the process as 'anaerobic composting', and some of the techniques that are suitable for home and garden use are included here, as the digestate possesses some characteristics that are similar to those found in compost and is a nutrient-rich fertiliser.

Composting was once the preserve of horticulturists and gardeners, providing a useful way of converting garden waste into a 'black gold' that would improve their soil. However, the increasing interest in the environment, sustainability and climate change has attracted a new type of composter, who sees composting as a means of protecting the environment by repurposing waste material that might otherwise be sent to landfill, and of reducing the greenhouse gases released into the atmosphere. The practice is now being actively promoted by local councils and environmental bodies as a means of treating organic waste from homes and business premises.

The Waste and Resources Action Programme (WRAP) regularly reviews the statistics relating to household food and drink waste and publishes current information on its website (wrap.org.uk/resources). According to research, organic materials make up about 60% of household waste, so the benefits of increasing the amount that goes to be composted could be considerable. Rural households tend to home compost (or burn) a higher percentage of their garden waste than urban households. It has been estimated that less than half of the rural garden waste generated is collected by the authorities, while urban households strongly rely on kerbside collections.

As councils have increased their charges for green waste collections, to help balance their books, there has been more interest in composting among urban households. However, showing an interest in composting is not enough. There is also a need to provide the right information to enable householders to compost successfully — and to continue composting. In 2004, for example, approximately 40% of householders who had bought a bin and started home composting gave up using it, because of a lack of knowledge. Almost two decades later, councils and others now produce leaflets, publish information online and train 'Master Composters' to provide support and advice. This has apparently resulted in a reduction in the drop-out rate to between 8 and 14%. In more recent years, this figure has reduced again, to 3.9%, which is probably about as low as it will go without further intervention.

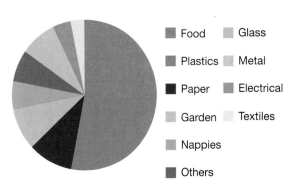

Domestic waste chart showing approximate proportions by type. Food is typically the largest group and as such should form the main target for environmentally concerned composters. The figures may vary year on year.

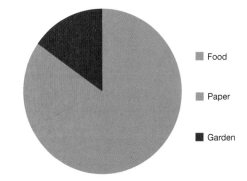

Most compostable domestic waste is comprised of food. Cooked food can be composted with a bin designed for that purpose or in an entry-level bin if pre-treated with bokashi.

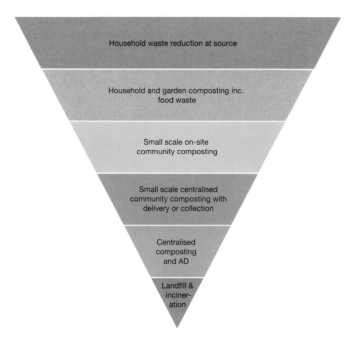

The compost hierarchy showing the preferred order for dealing with compostable waste. Waste reduction may not be applicable to organic material from the garden, making home composting the first environmental choice.

The amount of food waste sent for composting and anaerobic digestion is only a small proportion of the total waste collected. Almost half of the food waste in the average rubbish bin could have been composted, although the amount collected should increase with the spread of separate food waste kerbside collections. Unfortunately, much of the publicity material issued to home composters still states that cooked food cannot be home composted when in fact it is compostable if the appropriate techniques are used. Everyone, even apartment dwellers, can help to reduce the amount of waste sent to landfill or other more costly forms of treatment by composting some food and garden waste at home. Treatment of compostable waste at source has much to recommend it as it avoids the financial and environmental costs of kerbside collection.

Composting and Climate Change

Waste disposal results in the direct and indirect emissions of greenhouse gases (GHGs). The main gases are carbon dioxide (CO_2), methane (CH_4), nitrous oxide (N_2O) and non-methane hydrocarbons (NMHCs). Composting helps divert vegetable and other organic waste from landfill, in the process reducing the production of greenhouse gases, as well as helping prevent landfill disposal sites from filling up prematurely. When composting on the domestic front, nutrients found in organic material are recycled back to the soil, improving water retention and soil health. This leads to improved plant growth and sustainable food production.

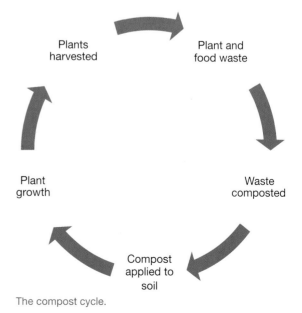

The compost cycle.

Plant matter buried with other waste in landfill and open stockpiles, such as manure heaps, results in anaerobic decomposition, which releases significant amounts of methane into the atmosphere. While this gas can be collected and burnt to generate electricity, it is a significant contributor to global greenhouse gas emissions, being 26 times more potent than carbon dioxide. Global emissions from waste have almost doubled since 1970 and now produce 3% of anthropogenic (human origin) emissions. About half of these emissions come from the anaerobic fermentation of solid waste disposed of on land. The global warming effect of anaerobic decomposition can be mitigated where the methane is collected and used to produce electricity, with carbon dioxide as a by-product. Although it is still a greenhouse gas, CO2 has a weaker global-warming effect than methane. It is the primary gas given off during aerobic composting, but this is not considered to affect global warming, as the materials decomposing are from what is known as the short-term carbon cycle. However, some greenhouse gases will still be produced, particularly during hot composting, if there is insufficient oxygen in some areas of the bin. This will lead to anaerobic decomposition occurring, resulting in the production of methane and nitrous oxide. It can be prevented by maintaining airflow and air spaces in the bin by ventilation, aeration and avoiding the material becoming waterlogged.

Although people may refer to anaerobic techniques as 'composting', strictly speaking the anaerobic process is more correctly described as anaerobic digestion or fermentation. Anaerobic fermentation in an enclosed anaerobic digester (AD) can be used to treat waste food, human effluent and livestock waste. The methane and other biogases produced in AD are collected and used for heating or power generation. Remaining bio-solids can be used as a fertilizer on farms. In hotter countries, small AD plants may be used to treat human waste from individual houses. Anaerobic composting on a bokashi system is used in agriculture and horticulture and can also be used in the garden and on a small scale in the home for kitchen waste (see Chapter 11).

Industrial composting practices that minimise anaerobic and maximise aerobic conditions are effective in reducing methane emissions from organic waste currently stockpiled or diverted from landfill.

Agriculture is a significant contributor to climate change, with at least 14% of global greenhouse gases (GHG) emitted as a result of farming activities, such as keeping livestock and ploughing, which releases carbon dioxide from the soil. The making and use of compost in farming, horticulture and home gardening contributes to the removal of atmospheric carbon through a process known as soil carbon sequestration. There is also an indirect contribution due to enhanced plant growth resulting from the use of compost on the soil. If as a result of applying compost fewer chemical fertilisers and pesticides are used, and the increased organic matter in the soil results in better water retention and a reduced need for irrigation, greenhouse gas emissions will be further reduced. Spreading compost and using a no-dig method can boost the carbon storage ability of the soil. While animal husbandry is a significant contributor to global warming it has been shown that, if compost is spread on grazing lands, it could capture a significant amount of greenhouse gas emissions with carbon storage utilising humus formation. The beneficial effect would continue into the future, resulting in an improvement of the overall greenhouse gas balance.

Table 1.1 Aerobic composting vs anaerobic digestion

Aerobic	Anaerobic
Requires oxygen for respiration	Does not require (or in the absence of) oxygen
Rapid decomposition	Slower decomposition
Produces heat (most noticeable in larger bins)	Generates little heat
Hot compost can kill pathogens, seeds and weeds	Insufficient heat to kill weeds or pathogens
No pungent gas produced	Pungent gas produced (for example, hydrogen sulphide)
Carbon dioxide is main gas released	Majority of energy released as methane
Produces compost	Produces sludge (digestate), which requires aerobic composting to complete process

The Intergovernmental Panel on Climate Change and the European Commission have formally recognised carbon sequestration in the soil as one of the measures through which greenhouse gas emissions can be mitigated.

Different Sites

Home and Allotment Composting

Aerobic home and allotment composting can make a valuable contribution to the reduction of the carbon footprint that is associated with the treatment of organic waste, by eliminating the road miles involved in collecting and taking the waste to the landfill tip or processing plant. Home composting also saves the road miles involved in transporting commercially produced compost to retailers and gardeners' homes. Landfilling of domestic organic waste is increasingly being replaced by industrial composting. While this is a welcome development, the collection and transport of the waste still involves avoidable road miles. In addition, home composting produces fewer methane emissions than commercial composting.

Individual householders, community gardens or schools may play only a small role in the processing of organic waste, with each using just one or two compost bins. However, it is likely that each plot-holder on an allotment, for example, will have at least one bin, with most having several, so an allotment site may be home to as many as 100 or even 200. The total area of land that could be involved in composting would be significantly increased if more gardens, lawns and parks were brought into use. Many county and city councils are responding to the climate emergency by actively promoting home composting, with subsidised compost bins and advice and training through Master Composter and similar schemes. Some are also adopting systems of composting and carbon sequestration in their parks and grounds, using the compost made from the green waste that they collect from households.

Today, more people live in cities or suburban areas than in rural areas, with limited outdoor space. Some urban dwellers may have a small garden with a lawn, or there will be a managed area of grass around an apartment block or commercial buildings and offices. In suburban areas, country towns and villages, the garden and grassed area will be larger. In both urban and rural areas, most householders who want access to more ground will live within a few miles of an allotment or community garden.

In terms of its environmental impact, the traditional garden lawn has not had a good press. Lawns can reduce biodiversity, and the pursuit of 'perfection' has tended to encourage the use of synthetic fertilisers and weedkillers. These can pollute the environment and have the unintended outcome of killing beneficial species. The mowing, fertilisation and general high level of maintenance necessary can result in a net

A moulded plastic bin is often the first type acquired by a composter.

Entry-level moulded bins. Composters will often use more than one type of bin.

Most composters start with one or two bins. Over the years they might expand to meet an increase in demand as their interest in composting develops.

Entry-level bins. A well-planned composting area can enhance the appearance of a working garden.

Biochar

Charcoal will be familiar to most people as a product of heating wood in the absence of oxygen. The term 'biochar' refers to the solid residue of plant material that has been pyrolysed, that is to say, carbonised under a high temperature. Biochar can be produced from almost any material, including bamboo, coco, straw, softwoods, hardwoods. The source of the organic content should be checked to ensure that it has not been grown or harvested in a way that damages the environment.

Biochar incorporation into soil can result in the removal of carbon dioxide from the atmosphere by terrestrial carbon sequestration. Biochar can be mixed with compost during the maturation period six to 12 weeks before it is applied to the soil. However, for the home composter, the main environmental benefits occur if biochar is mixed with a source of greens and introduced at the start of the composting process. This can result in reduced emissions of the greenhouse gases, methane, nitrous oxide and ammonia. The compost incorporating the biochar can be added to the soil when the composting process is complete, after three to 18 months.

Used in this way, biochar also acts as a bulking agent, helping to keep the compost aerated. It also results in an increase in temperature, leading to a consequent reduction in the time taken to produce finished compost.

emission of carbon dioxide and nitrous oxide, which are both contributors to global warming. However, the impact may be countered by the lawn's capability for carbon sequestration, especially if it is managed environmentally.

Community Composting

Concern for the environment and an increased sense of social responsibility have led to a significant growth in community composting schemes. These usually involve a community or group – an allotment, community garden, block of flats, community centre, café, village, workplace or school – coming together to turn the organic waste they produce into compost in a locally controlled, environmentally responsible, not-for-profit way. The resulting compost is then used locally. Community composters may also run education campaigns, promote home composting, and help others to establish new community composting schemes.

Community composting sites are covered by the waste regulations and need to meet the Environment Agency's requirements under the Environmental Permitting (England and Wales) Regulations. In the UK, a licence or an exemption certificate will be required. The exemption application granted to small-scale schemes is simple to obtain via the completion of an online application form.

The reception bins on the small-scale site for 60 plots at Stokes Wood Allotments, Leicester. Community composting is becoming more popular in the UK, with schemes covering allotment sites, community gardens and schools. Larger schemes may incorporate kerbside collection or drop-off by club members at the site.

The requirement for a permit or licence or an exemption will depend on two factors:

- the quantity of material stored on site at any one time; and
- the type of material accepted for composting and the time the material is stored on site until it is 'treated' – in other words, composted.

In a smaller community scheme, for example, on an allotment site where the organic garden material is produced and the compost is used on site by plot-holders or community gardeners, the material is usually processed in pallet bins. Some allotment- and village-based schemes can be open access, but this brings with it the risk that the reception bins will be overfilled as people leave waste for composting. Sometimes, excess waste may be dumped into the wrong bin because of a lack of space. In such situations the working area may need to be fenced off from the reception bins to avoid unsorted waste being added to the working bins. Alternatively, the scheme may be enclosed, which means that it will be open to receive waste only at certain times and under supervision. Community composting sites may also seek to promote composting to the wider public, by providing tours and training, and perhaps holiday activities such as painting compost bins to attract and educate children.

A school or allotment that wants to make compost on site from its own garden waste and uncooked fruit and vegetables, including children's snacks, for use on site, should be able to establish and operate the system at minimal cost. Usually, a series of low-cost domestic or pallet bins will be suitable. However, if a school or other workplace decides to compost catering waste from its kitchens, a more expensive composter such as the Ridan will be required, along with an increased level of planning and support. For more information on catering waste and food composting, *see* Chapter 6.

Where a community composting system is being established at a workplace, a tidy, more professional image may be important. In this case, more permanent bins made of sleepers, blocks or bricks may be used.

Reception bin overflowing into working bins at the Stokes Wood allotment site – maintaining a tidy site while providing open access can be difficult.

Community sites often have space for education and children's activities to promote composting.

A tour of the community composting site, with interest being shown in the aeration system in the Aerobin.

Community sites may include bins suitable for cooked food. On most such sites the bins will be bigger than these domestic models.

Larger community composting clubs and organisations may seek to set up a system whereby materials are collected and dropped off by members or acquired via kerbside collections. The finished compost may then be sold to members or to the public for off-site use. Many of these larger schemes will be grant-funded to cover ongoing operational or staff costs. However, the funding model does carry some risk as the income cannot usually be guaranteed in the long term.

Where a scheme is being set up to take waste from the local community, a Community Interest Company (CIC) should be formed to manage it, if the organising

Leaves deposited in community composting bins at a County Council site; the bins were originally used to compost waste from the offices.

society does not already have that status. Advice should be taken in advance to ascertain whether use as a composting site will require planning permission.

Country-House Composting

Allotment and community garden sites may be operated on a similar scale and use similar methods to professional gardeners caring for a large country-house or estate gardens. Traditionally, such sites would be based as a large-scale hot-composting system with three to five bins, either turning to aerate or operating on a non-turn system. It is well worth looking at such systems and the vegetable gardens when visiting National Trust houses and other similar properties. In most cases the gardeners are only too happy to explain the techniques used.

Bank of traditional bins on a soil base at a National Trust estate.

Part of a new composting facility at Blickling Hall in Norfolk, developed as part of a green initiative.

Principles

Composting: Aerobic and Anaerobic

Composting need not be complicated. Under the right conditions, it just happens. If left alone, all organic matter will naturally decompose, but composting means that the time taken can be reduced. The finished product will be in a form that allows the organic material and nutrients to be returned to the soil while minimising damage to the environment. There are some who define composting more narrowly as the aerobic decomposition of organic material and label the anaerobic process as digestion or fermentation. As a matter of convenience, the wider definition will be used here.

There are three different approaches to the home 'composting' of organic wastes: aerobic composting, vermicomposting and anaerobic digestion. (For more detail on aerobic and anaerobic respiration, *see* Chapter 3.)

- **Aerobic composting**: in this process, the waste is continually aerated by air flowing through the organic material and, optionally, by intermittent physical turning of the waste by the composter. There are two forms of composting, described as 'hot' or 'cold', depending on the temperatures reached during the process of decomposition.
- **Vermicomposting**: in this aerobic composting system, the organic material is eaten by worms and

is turned into compost as it passes through the worm's digestive system. The composting material is at, or about, ambient temperature with little temperature variation in the heap.
- **Anaerobic fermentation/digestion**: this process is carried out in an oxygen-deprived environment. It is used less frequently to deal with garden waste, but a bokashi system is often used as an indoor pre-composting treatment for food waste. The material being digested shows only a very slight increase in temperature.

Composters should be encouraged to try a variety of methods and techniques across the three approaches, to increase the range of materials composted. However, aerobic composting is the most popular of the three and the majority of this book will be devoted to the different techniques relating to this particular

Aerobic composting using a traditional heap.

Aerobic composting in entry-level moulded compost bins.

Aerobic composting in pallet bins with a lid and sliding hatch.

process. The advice on methods and techniques is intended to give guidance, but it is important to experiment using different methods and mixes of materials to determine those most suited to the waste available. In basic terms, if it works, it is being done right, no matter what others might say. It is also important to remember that working bins do not need to look pretty or smart in order to function, although keeping the site tidy does give a much more professional impression.

Health and Safety

Composting is a relatively low-risk activity and the risks that are present can be reduced to acceptable levels by a sensible assessment and the use of simple control measures. The hazards most likely to cause injury or ill health during composting, as with all gardening activities, will be those resulting from slips and falls, manual handling and the use of hand tools. However, the issue that probably causes the most concern in composting is the risk of infection. A number of disease-causing microorganisms may be

Microplastic Pollution

Pollution by microplastic particles is being recognised as an increasing environmental problem. Considerable publicity has been given to the issue of plastics in teabags contaminating the soil and watercourses. Also implicated are some of the materials used in gardening and composting, including woven polypropylene ground-cover fabric and old sheets of polythene that often serve to line and cover compost bins, heaps and windrows. The breakdown of such materials can cause environmental contamination, and this may also occur when waste materials are not sorted properly. Care should always be taken not to allow plastic-coated containers or food wrappings to end up in food waste and subsequently in the compost.

Some teabags still contain plastic and do not decompose properly when composted.

Magnification of a teabag after composting.

found in manure, compost and soil, and these could present a risk of infection – albeit relatively small – to the composter. These include the food-poisoning bacteria that are often featured in the press following an outbreak, such as salmonella, campylobacter, *Clostridia perfringens*, *E. coli*, and *Staphylococcus aureus*, as well as other pathogens present in the environment.

The risk from material from the domestic kitchen or garden is relatively low as it is less likely to be contaminated with animal and faecal waste than materials from some other sources. Luckily, most of the pathogenic bacteria, if present, will not be present in large enough numbers to cause disease in humans and in most cases the hot-composting process will kill those remaining. More details of these organisms are given in Chapter 4.

Bioaerosols (airborne microorganisms including bacteria and fungi spores) have been implicated in cases of infection in industrial composting plants, with rare cases associated with home gardening with compost. The number of bioaerosols will be dependent on the degree of contamination of the initial organic material, the growth of the organisms while awaiting composting, multiplication during the composting process and the actual activity being undertaken. Higher-risk activities include turning and sieving compost and any process that involves disturbing compost

on which mould is growing or when the compost smells mouldy.

The risks of infection when working with compost are small and a few simple precautions will reduce the likelihood to an acceptably low level:

- Wear gloves, either gardening gloves or nitrile/latex gloves for more delicate tasks. Wash or dispose of gloves after use.
- Wash hands and/or use hand sanitiser (if washing facilities are not available).
- Do not store compost in a greenhouse; it will warm up during the summer, allowing microorganisms to multiply.
- Open bags of compost slowly and in a well-ventilated space. When disturbing compost, do not hold the head directly over the bag or bin, to avoid breathing in any aerosols or spores that might be released.
- Moisten compost to reduce bioaerosols during turning (aeration) and consider wearing a dust mask (particularly if the compost smells musty).
- To avoid inhaling airborne particles when turning compost outdoors, stand up-wind so that they are blown away from the face.
- Anyone with a weakened immune system or lung diseases should wear a suitable face mask (FFP2 or N95 standard).
- Shred woody material in a well-ventilated area.

Compost bins on an allotment site. Trips, falls and manual handling incidents are the most likely cause of injury.

CHAPTER 2

COMPOSTING TECHNIQUES

With the range of different composting techniques available, the potential composter will need guidance when trying to select those that best suit their needs and lifestyle. The various aerobic composting systems all have their own pros and cons, and the information given here will help with choosing the most appropriate method for each situation. Details of anaerobic fermentation or digestion techniques are also given as, although these are not strictly speaking methods of composting, they do have their uses in treating kitchen and garden waste. More detailed information follows on entry-level methods for those new to composting, the use of more expensive bins and on hot composting and food-waste composting for those who wish to extend their activities, as well as more specialised techniques such as bokashi fermentation and composting with worms.

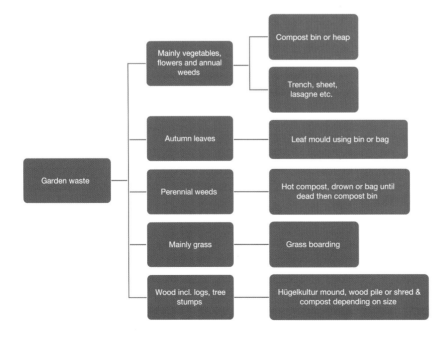

Options for composting garden waste.

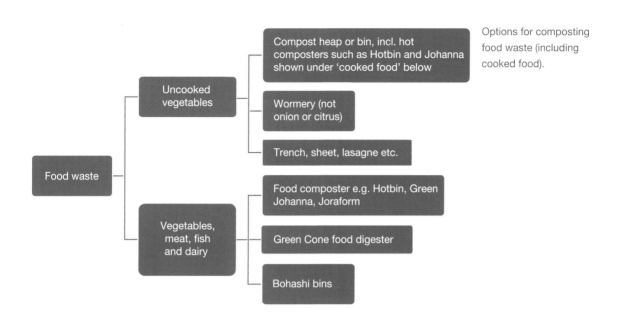

Options for composting food waste (including cooked food).

Table 2.1 Practical aspects of the different techniques

Compost system	Materials to be composted	Location	Composting time	Effort required
Aerobic composting (cold)	Fruit and vegetable peelings, non-fatty food waste, garden waste	Garden bin (indoors if small amounts)	Up to 18 months	Minimal. Add materials as available
Aerobic composting (hot)	Meat, fish and other food waste, fruit and vegetables, garden waste	Garden bin	1–12 months	Turning material during first month or as added
Trench, pit or post-hole	Fruit and vegetable peelings, food waste (meat, grains, dairy and cooked), garden waste	Garden, waste buried in trench or hole	Plant after 2–3+ months	Little other than digging and covering trench
Anaerobic fermentation (composting)	Kitchen and green garden waste	Garden, in covered heap	12 months	No turning
Anaerobic composting (bokashi)	Food and green waste, with the addition of bokashi bran	Indoors (bin) and outdoors to make pre-compost	10–14 days once bin is full	Compressing material as it is added, burying
Vermiculture (worm composting)	Kitchen and garden waste, non-fatty food waste	Wormery in garden, outbuilding or indoors	3–6 months	Feeding and maintaining worm bedding

Spreading or Burying, Mounds and Heaps

Sheet Composting, Trench and Post-Hole Techniques

Some methods require no expenditure or special equipment as the compost is made simply by spreading or burying the organic waste over the ground or adding it to a trench or post holes dug in the garden. As it is free and requires no equipment, it might be expected to be more popular than it is, but in fact these techniques are used only by a small minority of composters.

Sheet composting is best used for garden rather than kitchen waste. It can look untidy, but it is an effective way of adding organic material to large vegetable or allotment gardens and where no-dig techniques are being used. Trench composting is often used to provide a means of preparing the ground in the autumn for planting runner beans in the spring. Post-hole composting can be used to add organic material to small empty spaces or an already planted bed.

Pros: Inexpensive, no turning or aeration required. It is not visible once covered and feeds garden in situ. Post-hole composting can be used in permanent beds between plants.

Cons: There is a need to plan for future use of ground to ensure that space is available for the composting and growing. Digging is required. The waste

Lasagne composting in rows in a National Trust garden.

can take a long time to break down, and there is no compost to harvest. May be difficult to compost during winter months. Might attract rats and vermin if materials are not well buried. Composting meat or dairy products is not recommended.

Time required: 6–12 months

Lasagne Composting and Hügelkultur

Lasagne composting is a no-dig technique using layers of greens and browns and can also be used to fill raised beds.

The Hügelkultur method is a permaculture technique, with large pieces of decaying wood being used as a base and layers of compostable organic material added to form a mound up to several feet high. The wood and other materials are left to decompose below ground, while allowing the cultivation of plants on the raised mound, or less commonly a sunken bed. It may be considered as a combined raised (or sunken) bed and compost heap and is said to remain fertile for up to

Trench composting is often used as a seasonal technique during the late summer and autumn, with the waste being allowed to compost over a few months in preparation for spring planting.

Small Hügelkultur mound being built on a decaying wood base covered with layers of greens and browns. It will be topped with soil and ultimately planted up.

six years. The technique may be used to deal with tree stumps. There are more details of this technique in Chapter 5.

Pros: Provides an additional level on which to grow plants and a means of utilising rotting wood.

Cons: Forms a permanent mound so needs advance planning.

Compost Heap or Pile

The use of the traditional compost heap or pile has fallen out of fashion in the UK, as gardens have become smaller and many gardeners prefer to keep them neat and tidy. In these cases, a bin is a better option. However, a heap requires no expenditure, just a space in a less frequently used part of the garden that is suitable for a large pile of decomposing material that may

spread sideways in use. The pile may be extended to make a long pile or 'windrow'. Windrows of up to 5 or 6 feet in height and 8 or 10 feet at the base are often used to compost municipal organic waste. A heap can be used for both cold and hot composting and can be constructed using layers of browns and greens to give the correct ratio of carbon to nitrogen in the material being composted. This is referred to as the C:N ratio. Unfortunately, they also provide a readily available source of food and shelter for rats and other creatures, although regular turning may reduce the likelihood of them inhabiting the pile.

Pros: Inexpensive. No preparation required unless a concrete base is to be used. Easy to turn and aerate. Suitable for hot or cold composting. A heap is easy to monitor in terms of condition and the compost is easy to harvest.

Cons: May look messy and requires space as it may spread. Might attract rats and vermin. May be difficult to compost during winter months. Requires covering to prevent compost becoming waterlogged during wet weather. Not recommended for meat or dairy products.

Time required: 6–12 months

A traditional compost heap composting grass and leaves.

Traditional heaps have often been replaced by plastic and pallet bins.

A badly maintained heap spreading over the garden.

Compost in a wire bin. This type of bin is frequently used for making leaf mould.

Containers for Outdoor Composting

Moulded Plastic Bins

Plastic bins can be purchased in a range of shapes and sizes, the most popular of which (in the UK) are the 220- and 330-litre 'Daleks', sometimes available through subsidised local council schemes. Most of these bins will include a hatch for removing the finished compost. A base plate may also be available to help prevent entry of vermin.

These bins make excellent entry-level equipment. They are ready for immediate use, are long-lasting and can be moved easily when empty. Most are designed for the cold composting of uncooked kitchen and garden waste. The shape of the bin – narrower at the top than at the bottom – tends to make it difficult to turn the compost using a fork, but the material can be easily aerated using a compost aerator. Alternatively, the bin can be lifted off the collected and decomposing waste, which can then be mixed and returned to the bin. However, turning or aerating are not always necessary. If the mix, temperature and moisture content are

Basic plastic working compost bins on a busy allotment plot, pictured 'as found'.

right, the bins will attract worms that will do the turning on their own. (This is the case with all compost bins, except during the hot stage of hot composting.)

Once the compost is ready for use, the bin can be emptied by means of the hatch, if fitted, or by lifting the bin off the compost. If there is no hatch, or the bin is reluctant to move, it can be tipped over to make harvesting easier.

Pros: A moulded plastic bin is an excellent first bin, as it is relatively inexpensive and there is no assembly required. Solid sides provide good moisture retention (although it may dry out in hot weather). Designed for the easy cold-composting approach, with material simply being added as it becomes available.

Cons: Entry-level bins usually have a limited capacity; if the local council scheme offers a 'buy one get one half price' option, it is worth buying two of the larger 330-litre sizes. The small hatch makes access for harvesting more difficult than with the more expensive sectional versions. May dry out during hot weather. As they are light in weight, the bins or lid may blow away during windy weather if left partly full.

Time required: 12–18 months

Sectional Plastic Bins

Sectional bins tend to be straight-sided and larger than moulded bins. Most have solid side panels, but some are slatted, allowing for increased airflow.

Sectional bins tend to be easier to empty as they have a larger hatch. Some models use a rod system for holding the sides in place. The rod is lifted so that the bottom half of a side can be opened using the rod as a

Slatted versions of a sectional bin allow maximum ventilation but provide no insulation.

hinge. Sectional bins are available in a variety of shapes – square, octagonal and hexagonal. Many models include air vents to improve aeration and the sides are designed to offer some insulation. Bins of this type may have a two-part hinged lid. On some models, this is a weak point as the hinges may break with regular use.

Sectional bins are usually larger than the moulded types. This helps the composting material to retain heat, which means that they can be used for hot composting. They are usually more expensive than the moulded bins but well worth the investment for someone who is committed to composting. Most will require assembly. On the less expensive models the plastic may be relatively thin, and the bin may distort when fully filled.

Pros: Good range of sizes available. Easy to assemble and take apart, so they can be moved without much difficulty when empty. Most can be opened on any side providing easy access. The plastic sides of the bins may be designed to offer some insulation. Rectangular bins can be placed against walls, saving space and keeping the garden tidy.

Cons: Hinged lids may be broken with use or blown away in strong winds. More expensive than moulded bins but still good value for money. Bins placed against a wall may be on a rat run (*see* Chapter 8).

Time required: 12 months (cold composting) or 12 weeks or less for hot composting.

The Komp 250 sectional bin. Each side is in two sections held in place by a plastic rod down each corner.

A larger sectional bin is more suitable for a bigger garden.

Vertical (Gravity-Fed) Bins

Gravity-fed bins usually have three chambers, effectively combining a three-bin system in a single composter. They are more expensive than a simple bin and may not be suitable for gardens that produce a large quantity of compostable waste. The three chambers are stacked vertically so gravity can be used to turn and aerate the contents as they fall from an upper to a lower layer. This saves effort on the part of the composter turning the waste. Organic material is added to the top chamber and, after an appropriate time, the chamber floor is moved, allowing the material to fall to the next layer, and later from the second to third chamber. As with a tumbler bin, this is a closed composting system and moisture levels will need monitoring. The waste may need watering regularly to prevent drying out. It may be helpful to add an activator – for example, finished compost, comfrey or manure – to kick-start the decomposition of the first batches of organic material. A continuous cycle can be developed by regularly adding fresh material to the top chamber and removing compost from the bottom.

A gravity-fed bin system may be suitable for those with relatively small amounts of waste material, who do not need compost quickly. Examples include the Aeroplus 6000, in which the process in the first chamber is anaerobic to discourage fly infestation, and the Earthmaker.

Pros: Compact, so require little space. Gravity-fed, so the waste does not need turning manually. Tend to be easy to fill and harvest.

Cons: Expensive and not suitable where large quantities of waste are produced. The green:brown ratio needs to be correct at the time the material is added, as the bin is a closed system. May dry out. The material may need to be pushed from one level to the next.

Time required: claimed to be 3–4 months but some models may take longer.

Earthmaker gravity-fed bin.

Wooden Compost Bins

Traditional wooden bins have been used for years in home gardens and on allotments. The simplest and cheapest of this type of bin can be made by wiring three or four pallets together. Additional support can be given by screwing the pieces together and having separate corner posts driven into the ground.

Wooden bins, often known as New Zealand boxes, can be purchased in a wide range of sizes and prices. They may have solid sides for heat retention or slatted sides for increased ventilation. The front of the bin is usually removable, making it easier to turn and harvest the compost, or a three-sided bin can be used. When hot composting, a larger version of this style of bin is often used in a bank of three or four, with the composting materials being turned from one bin to the next as it is aerated. Wooden bins are also available in the shape of a beehive, which can be attractive in a smaller garden. These tend to be more expensive as they combine compost bin and garden feature.

Pros: Easy to make or assemble with low-cost bins available. Tanalised bins do not need regular treatment with preservative. Timber is a good insulator on solid-sided bins. Slatted versions provide less insulation but better ventilation.

Cons: The better-quality bins will be more expensive than a plastic bin. May need regular treatment with preservative unless tanalised. Slatted bins may dry out

A small wooden commercially available compost bin with slatted sides and removable front slats, offering good ventilation and easy access.

In larger gardens, a number of pallet bins can be used in a row, allowing waste to be turned from one bin to the next.

A three-sided layered pallet bin, left open at the front for ease of access when turning.

Home-made bins come in different shapes and sizes. Unusually, these are made out of plastic pallets.

An allotment row of three bins – the system involves turning material from one bin to another.

A Mantis metal tumbler, turned by means of a handle and mounted on a frame so that it can be emptied into a wheelbarrow.

Bins and netting enclosures being used to make leaf mould at the Stokes Wood allotment site.

more easily and weeds may germinate and grow between the slats.

Time required: ranges from a couple of months to two years, depending on technique being used (hot or cold composting).

Tumbler Composters

The tumbler type of bin is designed for the rapid composting of batches of waste. Aeration of the material is achieved by rotating or rolling the bin. They are available in plastic or metal and in a variety of designs, including a barrel-shaped version to be rotated vertically and a horizontal item resembling a tombola mixer, both of which are mounted off the ground on a frame. There are also a variety of ball- or barrel-shaped

bins that are turned by rolling. Some bins are insulated to help retain heat.

Some models have two chambers allowing two batches to be composted in the same drum. For rapid composting, the bins are best filled in a single batch. Tumblers tend to be relatively expensive, and some styles are heavy to turn when full. A cheaper plastic tumbler may not be as robust as a more expensive model.

Pros: Makes fast compost if material is added in a batch and turned regularly. Can be used in a paved area. Horizontal versions are easier to turn, and the metal versions are rodent-proof.

Cons: Need regular turning. Vertical tumblers can be heavy to turn when full as can the rolling versions. The handle on a loaded horizontal tumbler may swing back into place after turning, presenting a safety risk to a child using it. Contents may clump together.

Time required: varies with type; immature compost can be produced in a few weeks.

Compost Bins for Cooked Food

There are several domestic bins suitable for both garden and uncooked kitchen waste as well as cooked food. These bins are designed to be used to hot compost the waste at about 40–60°C, killing potential pathogens and weed seeds. They may be designed for composting waste in batches or require waste to be added once or twice a week. There are larger continuous throughput systems available, most of which require electrical power. However, some ranges popular with schools and cafés – for example, Joraform and Ridan – are hand-operated. For more information on this type of system, *see* Chapter 6.

Wormeries

Most commercially available domestic wormeries used in the UK are designed for kitchen waste (although there are versions sold for treating dog faeces, sold as 'dog poo wormeries'). The structure may have a single chamber for the worms and waste or three or four trays that are stacked one upon the other. A relatively new introduction is the Subpod where the chamber holding the worms is buried in the ground, allowing the worms access to the adjacent garden. Nearly all

The Jora (Joraform) horizontal insulated tumbler bin is suitable for composting the food waste from a large family.

above-ground models have a reservoir to collect the leachate ('worm wee'), which can be diluted and used as a liquid plant food. More details of wormeries and their use are given in Chapter 10.

Bins for Small or Hard-Landscaped Gardens

No garden is too small for some form of composting, even if it is completely hard-landscaped. Limited composting can even be carried out in an apartment or flat, particularly if it has a balcony; if not, indoor methods (*see* below) are still possible. A suitable composting bin or wormery can even make an appealing feature in a small garden, perhaps decorated by children or grand-children, or screened by a trellis or growing plants. A bokashi bin may be kept in a shed or storage container.

A conventional plastic bin that would normally be placed on soil can be purchased with a base plate or stood on plastic sheeting, cardboard or wood to reduce the risk of leachate staining concrete or timber decking. There are also small twin-chamber tumbler bins available mounted on a metal frame off the ground. In a small garden, wooden beehive-shaped bins are aesthetically pleasing and add interest.

A wormery provides an alternative to a compost bin and will normally be mounted on legs to lift the drain-age tap off the ground. There are small plastic wormeries commercially available that are suitable for

The Hotbin will compost cooked and raw food as well as garden waste at temperatures of 40–60°C or more.

A good first wormery: a stacking version consisting of a reservoir for 'worm wee' and two trays for worms.

An all-in-one wormery by Original Organics that has been in continuous use for about ten years.

kitchen waste, supplemented with shredded paper and cardboard, and may also be used on a balcony and even indoors. For more on wormeries, *see* Chapter 10.

Indoor Composting

It is not necessary to have a garden in order to become a composter. In the UK, indoor bokashi fermentation is frequently used in conjunction with subsequent aerobic composting in a 'Dalek', a 'soil factory' or a trench-composting set-up to complete the composting process. Indoor aerobic composting is also possible, although it is not commonly used in the UK.

In theory, any organic waste that can be composted outdoors can be composted indoors. In practice, however, items that compost slowly are best avoided, due to the limited size of indoor bins and the lower temperatures achieved inside them. Fruit and vegetables with a high water content, such as squash, and strong-smelling waste, such as onion, are also best avoided unless the container has a filter fitted. As with outdoor composting, if the waste material is cut to lengths of about 5cm (2in) or less, it will break down more quickly. Meat, dairy and fats are not suitable for composting aerobically in a conventional indoor or outdoor bin but can be treated in an indoor bokashi bin to produce pre-compost.

Shredded paper or cardboard are good carbon-rich browns for use in an indoor bin as they are easy to store and will not smell. More browns should be added every time greens are added.

Frequent aeration is necessary as the containers are not designed to provide a high level of ventilation. Mixing also breaks up lumps that might result in anaerobic fermentation and helps provide even moisture distribution. As indoor compost containers are relatively small, it is difficult to use most types of commercial compost aerator, but a long-handled hand fork makes an effective mixing tool.

A wide range of waterproof containers may be used for indoor composting, with plastic or metal being the most popular choice. It is best to have air holes drilled in the lid or around the top of the bin. If the bins are to be stacked to save storage space, the air holes should be drilled in the sides near the rim rather than in the lid. Drainage can be via holes in the bottom using a tray to catch the leachate, or a drainage tap can be fitted near the base of the bin. Small pebbles in the base can assist drainage. The container can be kept in any suitable room that has an easily cleaned floor.

The most commonly used containers in the UK are probably stackable plastic storage boxes or lidded buckets such as nappy buckets. The advantage of storage boxes is that they are available in a wide range of sizes, making it relatively easy to acquire a lidded compost bin of the right size for the space. In India, terracotta containers are often used. They make an effective container both indoors and in enclosed gardens and work especially well in places with temperature variations ranging from very hot and dry to cold. Using local pots also provides a livelihood to local potters.

It is better to have a bin that can be filled, sealed and set aside fairly frequently to avoid odours. Many people use 20-litre (5-gallon) containers, but larger containers of up to about 40 litres and even dustbins can be used. However, the larger the bin, the heavier it will be to move.

To prevent fruit flies and other flies from escaping, or getting into, the bin through the air holes, they should be kept small. If they are drilled close together, they can be covered with a piece of nylon screen, fine mesh garden netting or fine weldmesh glued to the inside of the container.

Terracotta bins on a terrace in Delhi, India. Excellent for small spaces.

An indoor bin can be loaded in the same way as an outdoor cold-composting bin, but the following technique has been adapted specifically for indoor composting:

1. Add a 10cm (4in) layer of soil or compost to the bin as a base layer.
2. Cover the base layer with a layer of shredded paper or newspaper.
3. Pre-mix kitchen vegetable waste with fresh browns before adding to the bin. A handful of soil or compost can be included in the mix.
4. Add materials as they become available or save and add weekly, at the same time carrying out aeration of the contents.
5. Cover the composting material with a layer of shredded paper or soil to reduce the number of fruit flies.

The contents should be given a final mix when the bin is full and then left for at least a week before being transferred to another container to mature until it is ready to use. This allows the original container to be reused.

Anaerobic 'Composting'

Strictly speaking, the term 'composting' applies only to decomposition by aerobic organisms and does not cover decomposition by anaerobes, which is more correctly referred to as 'fermentation' or 'digestion' (see Chapter 1). Brief details of different techniques are included here but, other than the use of bokashi to create pre-compost from cooked food, to make it suitable for vermin-free aerobic composting, most 'true' composters will use aerobic composting techniques.

Aerobic microorganisms are those that require oxygen for growth, respiration and reproduction. Aeration of the compost bin is designed to expose all the material being composted to oxygen, to help aerobic bacteria grow and function. The need to turn the compost in aerobic systems makes them more labour-intensive than those that rely on anaerobic digestion, although this is only the case where hot composting is being used – cold systems are often not manually aerated. The oxidation process that takes place in the compost heap releases some of the nitrogen and carbon dioxide from the organic material via evaporation, and of course leachate may be lost to the soil under the bin. Neither of these issues occur in a sealed container.

Anaerobes are bacteria that can survive without oxygen for growth. They will decompose organic material, but this will occur more slowly than with aerobes and create an unpleasant smell, due to the production, amongst other things, of hydrogen sulphide and amines (putrefaction). The process also produces methane, a greenhouse gas. For anaerobic composting a closed container, or a very restricted air supply is necessary to exclude the oxygen. Some home anaerobic composting methods are closed batch systems using airtight containers while others allow limited air access during the opening of the container to add new organic matter. Another system involves excluding air by covering the material to be composted with loose sand or water.

Bokashi

The bokashi method, the most common household indoor anaerobic system, is used to ferment kitchen waste, including cooked food. It uses specific strains of bacteria to produce a pre-compost that can then be added to a conventional compost bin or soil factory or buried straight into the garden. Two bins are normally used alternately, with one being filled while the other is fermenting. There is a need to buy, or make, a special bran.

With low-cost bokashi bins now available in the UK, it is well worth giving bokashi a try alongside a main bin (for example, a 'Dalek') being used for cold composting. In a very small garden, the pre-compost produced by the bokashi bin can be added to a soil factory to convert to a material that can be used to top up patio pots. Bokashi can also be used on the farm or in the allotment. Further information is given in Chapter 11.

Bag or Sack Anaerobic Composting

Composting in a sealed bag or sack is sometimes used where the householder does not have a garden or space for a compost bin, as the sacks can be stored in a small outdoor space or in a shed or garage. It may also be a way of composting kitchen waste during the

Bokashi, an indoor anaerobic system suitable for kitchen waste, including cooked food.

Bokashi bin: compressing the food waste and bran to remove air pockets.

A soil factory that can be used to convert pre-compost from an indoor bokashi bin by mixing it with soil in another indoor container.

A small bokashi windrow heap on the Stokes Wood demonstration site, completely wrapped in plastic sheeting to exclude air.

winter. The disadvantage is that it will entail saving the waste in a bin, or other leak- and smell-proof container, until there is enough to fill the bag in one go, combining with the browns. It could be argued that anaerobic composting in a bag or sack requires less work than conventional composting as the contents do not need to be aerated by turning at regular intervals, but it will smell.

The simplest method is to put the kitchen waste in a thick plastic bag such as an old compost or builder's refuse bag. The organic material is soaked before the bag is sealed. As a safety measure, double-bagging is recommended to avoid the full bag splitting when being handled. It is easier to put one bag inside the other *before* filling with organic material. As it helps the composting process to turn the bags occasionally, it is important to choose a size of bag that is relatively easy to handle. Although 100- to 150-litre bags can take a good amount of material, they might be too heavy to handle when full, so 70-litre bags might be more suitable. It is important to ensure there are no holes in the bags. Air must be prevented from entering the mix as the objective is to achieve anaerobic conditions.

'Composting in a bag' is usually treated as a batch composting system, with materials being set aside separately until the bag can be fully filled and secured. Nitrogen-rich wet material should be mixed together with a roughly equivalent quantity of greens and browns. Some composters recommend the addition of commercial compost activator, active compost from a compost heap or garden soil, to boost the fermentation process by introducing microbes to the bag. If filling the bag with alternate layers of greens and browns, active compost, commercial compost activator or soil can be sprinkled over every layer of the greens. Rather than using equal parts of greens and browns, soil can be added as a third component, using one-third compost or soil, one-third greens and one-third browns.

When the bag is full, the material is soaked with water and the surplus air squeezed out of the bag. The bag is then sealed by tying or taping, to prevent the access of air.

Ideally, the bag should be turned every couple of weeks to mix the materials. Turning is made easier if the bags are put into a plastic barrel that can be put on its side and rolled with minimum effort. This also protects them from physical damage. The bags or barrel should be left in a sunny spot during the summer and preferably in a heated or frost-free shed or garage during the winter.

The time taken to produce compost in an anaerobic bag varies according to the mix and conditions. In a sunny spot, compost will be ready in eight weeks to six months, while in colder positions the fermentation will take longer. When the process is complete, the material should look and smell like normal compost. If it is left undisturbed for about a year it will produce garden-ready compost, which should be free of pathogens; storing is recommended if there is a likelihood of pathogens being present in the original feedstock. Where the original materials are likely to have been pathogen-free, the immature compost can be harvested after a few weeks. However, anaerobic compost will be acid and will need to be finished off with an aerobic stage before being used for plants. It can be stored under aerobic conditions for a least a month before use, to allow it to lose its acidity. Alternatively, it can be spread and dug into the soil in a fallow area of the garden or allotment. The soil should be ready for use after two to four weeks. Its suitability can be confirmed by checking the pH.

Barrel or Bucket Anaerobic Composting

This simple method of anaerobic composting uses a lidded bottomless barrel or bucket sunk into the ground as a digester. The bottom of the barrel is buried 15–30cm (6–12in) deep in the garden. A bucket should be set slightly deeper, to keep it stable. Weldmesh can be put across the bottom to exclude rats.

In poorly draining soils, the hole can be dug larger than the size of the barrel or bucket, and the gap filled with a pebble and soil mix to help drainage. On heavy clay, the barrel can be positioned on a mound or mounted above the ground, in which case, the bottom of the barrel is not removed. The mound should be built of soil and pebbles and held in place by logs, boards or stones. An above-ground barrel digester, with drainage holes drilled in its base, can be raised on bricks, at a height that allows a tray or other container to be slid underneath, to catch the leachate. Ideally, the tray should be just smaller than the base of the bin, to prevent it filling with rainwater.

In use, the digester is filled with nitrogen-rich organic waste, such as kitchen waste, coffee grounds and filters, compostable teabags and grass clippings. Carbon-rich materials are best avoided as they will slow the process. Once in the barrel, the waste is compressed to remove any extra air and the lid fitted in place. It is best composted using a batch system with

the bin being filled periodically. If a top-up system is being used and the feedstock is not added all in one go, fresh material should be added on as few occasions as possible, as every time the bin is opened air is allowed in. The contents should be watered often – they should be kept wet rather than just moist. A slimy consistency and slight odour of sulphur due to anaerobic fermentation may be a warning in aerobic composting, but they are a good sign in an anaerobic system.

The container should be left sealed and undisturbed for at least eight weeks for immature compost. This should then be allowed to mature under aerobic conditions for between two months and a year. In practice, several barrels will be required to provide a means of dealing with waste throughout the year.

Covered Static Compost Heap

The covered heap is a variation of anaerobic fermentation that relies on the use of water to exclude oxygen from the material. The heap should be at least 120–150cm (4–5ft) wide and about 90cm (3ft) high and laid on freshly dug soil soaked with water. It is then built in the normal way, soaked and covered by a black plastic sheet. Water replaces air in what would normally be the air spaces in the mix. Soil is placed around the edges to make a seal and exclude as much air as possible.

The objective is to maintain a moisture level of 70% or more, rather than the normal 40 to 60%. The moisture content can be tested by squeezing compost in the hand; water should run freely out of the compost, rather than it having the wrung-out sponge effect that is sought when aerobic composting.

Covering the plastic with a tarp will help protect it from physical damage. The heap should be left undisturbed for two to three months to produce immature compost.

Anaerobic Composting Using a Bin

In a variation of the covered-heap method, a New Zealand or pallet bin can be used to retain the compost. The bin should have solid sides and should be covered with thick plastic to retain moisture and exclude air. This can be held in place by a boarded lid, which fits inside the wooden sides of the bin and rests

Small anaerobic heap, covered in polythene to exclude air and protected from potential damage to the polythene by a heavy-duty tarp.

on the plastic sheet covering the top of the organic material.

The moisture content will need to be monitored regularly to maintain the desired level of 70% or more, with additional water being added if necessary. During this process the cover(s) will need to be removed, exposing the surface to air, but watering will fill any air spaces that form among the material, recreating anaerobic conditions. With this type of composting, a wet slimy texture and unpleasant smells are good signs, indicating anaerobic decomposition.

Submersion or Underwater Composting

Submersion composting has the advantage of reducing any unpleasant odours, as the chemical reactions take place under water. The materials to be composted are put in a suitably sized container, covered with water, and allowed to decompose. Submersion composting usually takes longer than other methods, as the water acts as a cooling agent, slowing the metabolism of the composting microbes.

CHAPTER 3

COMPOSTING: PROCESS AND THE REQUIRED CONDITIONS

Basic Requirements of the Composting Process

Composting is the biological aerobic decomposition of solid organic material using naturally occurring organisms to produce a humus-like substance. By properly managing the basic requirements of the composting process – air (oxygen), moisture, nitrogen (greens), carbon (browns), pH and temperature – to produce the optimum conditions for the composting organisms, the composter can influence both the speed of the process and the quality of the compost produced. Active (hot) composting generates a considerable amount of heat, together with carbon dioxide and water vapour, which can amount to half the weight of the initial organic materials.

This chapter will introduce some of the science of composting and the stages of decomposition of the organic waste in which the organic molecules in the food and plant materials are converted by biological decomposition into the dark humus-like substance that is compost. The compost heap is home to a complex ecosystem in which the physical heap provides air, water and food for the organisms undertaking the decomposition and the skilled composter ensures that these are provided in a readily

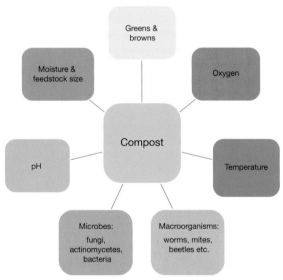

The conditions necessary for aerobic composting.

available form throughout the process. In order to develop the necessary skills, it will be useful for the composter to have an understanding of the three levels of decomposition and the two main categories of organisms involved: the physical and chemical decomposers.

The three levels of organisms involved in composting.

Organisms Involved in Decomposition

First-Level Decomposers

These chemical decomposers are mostly microscopic microorganisms that secrete enzymes which break down more complex organic compounds while their cells absorb simpler compounds. Sugars, starches and proteins are converted to water, energy and carbon dioxide, while nutrients such as nitrogen and phosphorus are released. The organisms play the major role in the composting process. They use the organic matter – leaves, grass clippings, vegetables and other plants – food scraps, and the bodies and excrement of soil invertebrates in the compost bin or heap as a source of food, resulting in its decomposition to the rich brown material known as compost.

The natural decomposition process can be accelerated by providing the optimum conditions for the soil microorganisms to break down the waste more quickly than would occur without intervention. The skill lies in providing them with the carbon they require for energy, nitrogen to build proteins, oxygen for respiration, moisture, and so on.

About 80 to 90% of the microorganisms found in compost heaps are bacteria, which, together with fungi and actinomycetes, break down the organic material chemically, in contrast to the physical action of the macroorganisms. The actual species of composting microorganism in any given heap will vary, depending on the climate, moisture content, pH, temperature and the conditions within the particular part of the heap from which the sample is taken.

Second-Level Decomposers

Physical decomposers are mostly macroorganisms that can be seen with the naked eye, but may also be observed in detail with a hand lens or stereoscopic microscope. Those classified as second-level decomposers – for example, springtails, nematodes, beetle mites, mould mites and protozoa – eat the organic matter and the organisms that make up the first-level decomposers.

Third-Level Decomposers

The third level of decomposers that work to produce compost are larger. They physically break down the organic material by chewing, tearing and, in some cases, sucking it into smaller pieces. Ants, beetles, centipedes, 'composting' worms, flies, millipedes, slugs, snails, spiders and woodlice (sow bugs) are all in this group and can easily be seen by the naked eye. Searching for and identifying these mini beasts using a hand lens or microscope attached to a laptop provides an excellent introduction to composting for adults and can be a fun educational activity for primary schoolchildren.

Requirements for Effective Composting

Oxygen and Aeration

An aerobic composting process consumes large amounts of oxygen. During the first days of composting, the more easily degradable components of the organic materials are rapidly metabolised. The need for oxygen and the production of heat are greatest during these

Aeration created by turning compost manually into an adjacent bin using a manure fork.

early stages and then decreases as the process continues. If the supply of oxygen is limited, the composting process slows and the process becomes anaerobic (without oxygen). A minimum oxygen concentration of 5% within the pore spaces of the composting material is recommended for a well-managed compost facility (air contains about 21% oxygen).

In addition to providing oxygen, aeration removes heat, water vapour and other gases from within the composting materials. In fact, the required rate of aeration in terms of heat removal can be 10 times greater than for supplying oxygen. Effective aeration increases the rate of composting, helps control the temperature and enables aerobic microbe growth. It can be achieved passively, using particle size and air spaces within the heap. This works best if a route by which air may enter the bin is created – lifting a solid-sided bin off the ground using, for example, a pallet as a base; adding a layer of twigs, stalks and browns; or by physical turning or mechanical mixing. Oxygen can also be provided by drilling air holes and inserting ventilator pipes or poles within the heap. Letting the worms turn the compost is another form of passive aeration, with these useful creatures doing the turning rather than the composter.

When hot composting, turning and mixing the contents during the first three or four weeks does have the additional advantage of loosening the mixture. Building the bin using wire or slats with a gap between them is favoured by some composters, as it improves ventilation, allowing air to enter the bin between the slats to

supplement that rising from the base. However, this can also increase evaporation and reduce the temperature of the contents.

When cold composting is being carried out in a plastic bin, the compost can be aerated using a compost aerator. This is a special tool with a metal rod/handle and hinged metal arms with teeth on the end that is pushed into the compost and then pulled out. The teeth will open out as it is withdrawn, creating air pockets inside the compost. Another type of aerator has a large corkscrew on the end, which is turned into the compost. While tools of this type do not aerate the bin as effectively as turning all the contents with a fork, they do break up any matted waste or lumps that may have encouraged anaerobic organisms. A broomstick can also be used to make air holes.

Passive aeration: a base layer of twigs, brassica stalks, and so on, enables air to enter at the bottom of the bin and flow up through the air spaces in the organic material.

A slatted bin is favoured by some composters for passive aeration, which is created by air entering between the slats.

A wire bin is often used instead of a slatted bin.

Removing a hand-operated auger from the compost can be hard work but models are available to fit an electric drill.

The central aeration cone in an Aerobin 400 removes the need to turn the compost. A plastic pipe, or pipes, with holes drilled in it can be used as a home-made ventilator.

'Corkscrew' compost aerators require little effort and can be used to remove a small compost sample for monitoring moisture levels in the bin. They are also suitable for use in plastic compost bins.

Using most aerators requires less effort than turning with a fork. This may not be true of an auger, such as that shown.

A sample of compost being extracted using a corkscrew aerator.

Winged aerators are pushed or stabbed into the compost, then the wings open as the aerator is removed. Those with small wings are easier to pull out of the compost, but larger wings aerate a bigger area.

A small single-chamber tumbler bin. Turning the bin aerates the compost, creating air spaces and possibly resulting in faster composting.

Removing a winged aerator from the compost.

The central rod inside a tumbler bin helps break up the compost when the bin is turned.

Tumbler compost bins are designed to aerate the organic material when they are turned. The aeration is usually carried out by a central rod that breaks up the waste during turning. Using a tumbler bin creates increased aeration, allowing the composting process to be accelerated with less physical effort.

Temperature

The temperature of the heap or bin is not of great importance when cold composting, as it will be dependent on the ambient air temperature. It may rise for a few days when large amounts of green material are added, but this will not have a significant effect. However, when hot composting, it is the temperature that will determine the speed and effectiveness of the compost process. It will also frequently determine how much and how often aeration is required. Most new composters start by using cold-composting methods and many move on to hot-composting techniques as their knowledge and skills develop. The choice of technique will also influence the practical conditions that will be required.

Composting is most efficient when the temperature of the composting material is within the two temperature ranges known as mesophilic 26–48°C (80–120°F) and thermophilic 40–65°C (105–150°F). Mesophilic temperatures allow effective composting, but many experts recommend maintaining the temperature in the higher thermophilic range, because these temperatures destroy more pathogens, diseases, weed seeds and insect larvae in the composting materials. The PAS 100 regulations have set the critical temperature for killing human pathogens at 65–80°C (150–176°F) for a specified time, which should destroy most plant pathogens as well. The critical temperature for destroying most weed seed is 63°C (145°F).

Microbial decomposition during composting releases large amounts of energy as heat, and the insulating qualities of the composting materials lead to an accumulation of this heat, raising the temperature of the bin or heap. The materials lose heat as water evaporates and as air movement carries away the water vapour and other gases. Turning and aerating a compost pile accelerates the heat loss in the period immediately after aeration, so this can be used to reduce the temperature. Following the initial temperature drop it will increase again, so turning can be used to prolong the time the bin is at operational temperature. Cold-composting techniques require less effort, but temperatures that favour thermophiles may be reached only in limited parts of the heap after new material is added. Most of the heap will not exceed 40°C and it

is the mesophiles, not thermophiles, that will do most of the work (see Chapter 4). Useful compost will be produced but pathogens, weeds and seeds will survive in it.

The optimum temperature for tiger worms is 20–25°C (68–77°F) so, as the temperature rises, the worms will migrate to cooler areas of the organic material – the top and lid of the bin – or leave the heap completely until it cools. This means that worms cannot be relied upon to turn the compost during the hotter stages.

Heat accumulation in a compost pile can rise above 70°C (160°F) because of the heat generated by microbial activity and the insulating qualities of the composting materials. When the temperature reaches this level, many of the microbes die or become dormant. The composting process will effectively stop and will not recover until the population of the microorganisms is re-established.

The compost temperature can be easily monitored using a compost thermometer, which has a long probe that reaches into the deeper regions of the bin or heap. The most common probes measure between 300 and 500mm (12–20in). The longer probes are more flexible, in that they can be used on large and small bins, while the shorter ones are suitable for small to medium

Table 3.1 Additional conditions required for hot and cold composting

	Cold Composting	Hot Composting
Temperature	Not relevant, but normally ambient or just above. May briefly heat up following the addition of grass or other greens that decompose quickly	Reaches 50–65°C in two to three days; can be maintained at 40–60°C range
Bin or heap size	Size unimportant; can range from a bucket to a large compost bin	Ideally at least 1 sq m by 1.5m high
Material added	As produced, in equal parts greens and browns over the composting period	In layers of greens and browns to fill whole bin in one batch if possible
Aeration required	Turning the active top layers will speed the process	Turning the contents every two days for the first two weeks will speed the process and help maintain the temperature required. Alternatively, turn weekly or two or three times during the composting period
Time taken	1–2 years	2–12 weeks, plus maturation period
Harvesting	Bottom layers harvested via a hatch or by lifting the bin off the compost	All the contents are ready at the same time
Kills weed seeds and pathogens?	No	Yes

compost heaps or bins. Many have dials which show the temperature in both Celsius and Fahrenheit and have markings to indicate when the compost is at the optimal temperature. Readings should be taken at several points in the bin. The temperature can also be estimated by leaving a fork in the decomposing material until it has reached the temperature of the pile and then removing it and feeling the prongs. This is an acquired skill.

When the composting material becomes too hot, heat loss should be accelerated by forced aeration or by turning. Since most of the heat loss during composting results from the evaporation of water, the materials should not be allowed to dry below 40% moisture. Low moisture increases the chance of high temperature damage and spontaneous combustion.

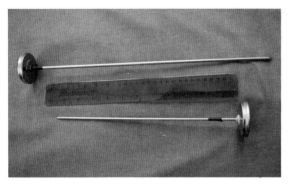

Most compost thermometers will have a probe length of between 300mm and 500mm (12in and 20in), so that the temperature can be recorded in the central core.

Hot-composting bin. The temperature after one or two days will reach 40ºC, the top of mesophilic range, and be entering the thermophilic.

After three days the temperature will have reached 49ºC, well into the hot thermophilic stage. It should be turned every second day, or if the temperature falls, to maintain the contents within the thermophilic range.

Fungi growing in a lidded compost bin at 40ºC.

Moisture

Moisture is the lifeblood of the metabolic processes of the microbes. Water provides the medium for chemical reactions, transports nutrients and allows the microorganisms to move from place to place. In theory, biological activity is optimum when the materials are saturated, but at moisture levels above 60% water displaces much of the air in the pore spaces of the composting materials. This limits air movement and leads to anaerobic conditions. Conversely, activity ceases almost entirely below a moisture content of around 15%. Moisture content generally decreases as the organic material decomposes. If required, moisture can be added at the shredding stage to be blended with the processed materials.

Efficient activity is encouraged when the moisture is maintained at between 40% and 60%. Ideally, this will be achieved when the materials are thoroughly wet but not waterlogged or dripping excessive water. Moisture content can be measured and recorded as part of the PAS 100 compost protocol, but the home composter can also estimate it by using a meter or by means of the 'sponge test'.

The sponge test involves squeezing and releasing a handful of the compost and noting the effects, as follows:

- If the compost does not form a ball when squeezed and released, the moisture content is likely to be around 40% or less.
- If it forms a ball but falls apart when released, the moisture is probably in the range of 40–50%.
- If it forms a ball and stays intact when released, looks damp and expels a few drops of water, it will be in the range of 50–60%.
- If water runs freely from the squeezed compost, it is too wet and probably at 65% or more.

Sponge test: at a moisture content of 40–50% the compost will form a ball when squeezed but fall apart when released.

Combined moisture and pH meters. A moisture meter can be used to supplement the sponge test during composting, while a combined instrument allows pH to be monitored as well.

At a moisture content of 50–60% the compost will produce a few drops of water when squeezed and stay in a ball when released.

Monitoring moisture content. Meters will often have colour-coded or numerical zones rather than provide a direct reading. The cheap models may not be accurate but can provide an indication as to when a sponge test may be appropriate without disturbing the heap.

Carbon, Nitrogen and Other Nutrients

The balance of nutrient concentrations during the composting process can have a significant influence on the quality and value of the end product. The focus during composting tends to be on the ratio of carbon to nitrogen (the C:N ratio), but phosphorus (P) and potassium (K) are also primary nutrients required by the microorganisms involved, and nitrogen, phosphorus and potassium (N-P-K) are the primary nutrients for plants. Excessive or insufficient carbon (browns) or nitrogen (greens) will have a negative effect on the process. Carbon provides microorganisms with both energy and growth; nitrogen is essential for protein and reproduction. In general, biological organisms need about 25 times more carbon than nitrogen, so it is important to provide carbon and nitrogen in appropriate proportions.

Raw materials blended to provide a C:N ratio of 25:1 to 30:1 are ideal for active composting, although initial ratios over a wider range of 20:1 up to 40:1 consistently give good results. With C:N ratios below 20:1 the available carbon is fully used without stabilising all the nitrogen. The excess nitrogen may be lost to the atmosphere as ammonia or nitrous oxide, and odour can become a problem. Mixes with C:N ratios higher than 40:1 require longer composting times for the microorganisms to use the excess carbon because of the absence of available nitrogen. Based on this science, as a general guide when using a layered bin, layers of about 7.5cm (3in) greens to 2.5cm (1in) brown give a good C:N ratio. The browns, such as shredded paper, cardboard, woodchip and autumn leaves, form a dense layer, while the greens, such as garden weeds and vegetables, are more voluminous.

In practice, many composters find that an approximate 50:50 mix of greens and browns works well enough when cold composting. In any case, the ratio can easily be adjusted during use.

Table 3.2 Greens and browns: ratios of selected materials. Information from *On-Farm Composting Handbook* and other sources

Material	C:N	Material	C:N
Fish scraps	2.6–5:1	Fresh leaves	37–85:1
Poultry manure	3–10:1	Mushroom compost	40:1
Pig manure	6:1	Leaves (dry)	47:1 (60:1)
Humus	10:1	Newspaper	50–200:1
Hair/fur	10–15:1	Corn cobs	56–123:1
Alfalfa	12:1	Peat moss	58:1
Sheep manure	13–20:1	Manure (horse) and straw	60:1
Vegetable trimmings/scraps	12–25:1, 11–13:1	Pine needles	60–100:1
Food scraps/ kitchen waste	15–17:1	Tissue paper	70:1
Grass clippings	17–20:1, 9–25:1	Straw/hay	75–100:1
Seaweed	19:1	Paper towel	110:1
Coffee grounds	14:1, 20–25:1	Office paper	129:1
Cow manure	20:1	Bark (softwood)	131–1285:1
Fresh weeds	20:1	Sawdust (weathered)	142–625:1
Clover	23:1	Woodchip (soft wood)	226:1
Horse manure	25:1	Cardboard (shredded)	350–378:1
Ashes, wood	25:1	Twigs (small)	500:1
Green leaves (oak)	26:1	Sawdust (fresh)	500–600:1
Fruit waste	25–49:1	Cardboard (corrugated)	563:1
General garden waste	30–40:1	Wood chips and twigs	700:1
Nut shells	35:1		

Cut grass is an excellent green that heats up quickly, so must be used with plenty of browns.

Office paper is a good brown. It is best shredded and can be soaked before being added to the bin. It tends to clump less if it is added in a thin layer and then watered.

Hair is a more unusual green, but it contains about 10–15% nitrogen. It may be possible to acquire dog hair collected from a vacuum cleaner.

Cardboard is a good source of carbon. Cardboard boxes can be shredded or torn into easily compostable pieces.

Wool contains 10% nitrogen, so packaging made from wool can be torn into pieces and used as a green.

Any tape should be removed from cardboard boxes before composting.

Autumn leaves as a brown layer. Dry leaves have a C:N ratio of 47–60:1, making an excellent brown.

If a non-layered system is being used, greens and browns should be well mixed when added to the bin.

Feedstock particle size

As microbial activity resulting in decomposition generally occurs on the surface of the organic particles, degradability can be improved by reducing the particle size. This increases the surface area, but it also introduces the risk of diminishing porosity. When the particles are too small, they become compacted, restricting airflow through the bin and preventing the entry of the required oxygen. This can be a problem with items such as sawdust.

Some shrinkage will also occur during the composting process, as the organic materials settle in the bin and become more compacted. This is particularly noticeable when cold composting, where the finished material can shrink by as much as a third.

Root crops and many vegetable stalks will compost more quickly if chopped into small pieces and crushed to increase the surface area exposed to microbial activity.

Brassica stalks cut to about 8cm (3in or so); in practice they can be left longer.

Feedstock root crops ready to be layered in a beehive bin.

Fruit stones hammered and ready for composting.

A shredder is recommended for woody material, such as the material pruned from shrubs. A small electric one will be adequate for home use; larger equipment can be hired if necessary.

Fruit stones are slow to compost unless smashed. A large hammer crushes them easily enough.

Elder ready for composting after shredding in a small electric shredder.

Garden shears are useful for cutting material; if they have long handles, that will reduce the need for bending.

The chopping shafts in the chopper-mixer, and some of the end product.

Pumpkins are probably best cut up with a spade. The seeds may survive cold composting.

Material waiting to be composted at a National Trust garden.

Tractor bucket, bags and a pile of grass waiting to be used at a National Trust property.

Chopper-mixer at the National Trust's Blickling Hall in Norfolk. This type of equipment can be used to speed up the composting of green waste.

Material cut into short lengths is easier to turn manually, but where mechanical turning is available, and the material can be composted for up to a year, it can be left longer. This will save the composter quite a lot of time!

Testing the pH of Compost

The pH scale is used to measure the acidity and alkalinity of solutions. On the scale of 0 to 14, those with a pH of less than 7 are acidic, those with a pH of 7 are neutral, and those with a pH greater than 7 are alkaline.

Measuring the pH of compost provides a means of monitoring the decomposition process. Compost microorganisms operate best under neutral to acidic conditions, with the normal pH range of a heap being between 5.5 to 8. It tends to be acidic during the early stages due to the formation of organic acids and then moves to a slightly alkaline pH during the composting. Mature compost has a pH of between 6 and 8. If the pH is acidic at any time other than during the initial stages, this may indicate anaerobic conditions, which would require action to be taken.

Electronic pH Meter

The best option for measuring pH is an electronic soil/compost pH meter. Basic models are readily available from garden centres and are adequate for the task, but a more expensive and accurate 'field test' instrument might be more suitable in many cases, for example, at a community composting site.

pH Papers or Strips

Testing papers or strips can be purchased covering different pH ranges, and 4.5 or 5 to 10 is ideal for testing compost, as it is easier to distinguish between slight differences in colour. If the compost is sufficiently moist, it should be possible to take a direct reading by simply inserting the end of the strip into the compost for a few minutes to absorb the water. However, when using a test strip, chemical dye and some meters, it might be more efficient and accurate to mix the compost with distilled water or a buffer solution before testing.

Soil Test Kits

Soil test kits for determining the soil pH can also be used for compost samples. They use-coloured dyes that are mixed with the compost in water and the resulting colour is compared to a chart to read the pH level.

Composting Microorganisms

Certain microbes are the key workers involved in all methods of making compost. They also play a role in producing the temperature changes that are necessary to achieve effective hot composting (for more on this, *see* Chapter 4).

Bacteria

Bacteria are small, single-celled organisms. They are the dominant population of microorganisms during all stages of the composting process, with between 1 million and 1 billion present per gram of compost. They are particularly active in the breaking down of the

pH of mixed garden waste is between 5 and 7. May turn slightly acidic during initial stages	**Mature compost**	May level off at between 8.0 and 9.0 towards end of the process

0	1	2	3	4	5	6	7	8	9	10	11	12	13	14

⬅ **Acidic**	**Neutral**	**Alkaline** ➡

Being able to measure the pH is important in composting.

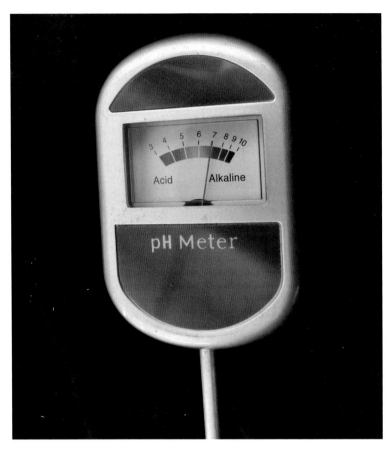

Recording compost pH, showing a reading of just under 7. The initial pH of home compost may be slightly acid, between pH 5 and 7, while the pH of finished compost is normally in the range pH 6–8.

easily degraded organic material, whereas the actinomycetes and fungi (see below) typically proliferate in the later stages.

Bacteria require carbon (browns) and nitrogen (greens). They use carbon as a source of protein and nitrogen as their main source of energy.

Most bacteria are spherical (cocci), or rod-shaped (bacilli). They may be observed through a digital microscope, stereoscopic or general laboratory microscope.

Actinomycetes

Actinomycetes are also bacteria, but they are generally discussed separately as they play a major role in the decomposition of the less easily degraded materials. Actinomycetes can also tolerate drier conditions than many bacteria and produce a chemical (geosmin) that is responsible for the typical musty, earthy smell of compost. They are normally found in compost five

to seven days after the start of the process. The mesophilic actinomycetes operate best in areas of medium temperature (20–50°C) in the compost, normally at the edges of the heap or bin and at the end of the process. Thermophilic actinomycetes grow at between 30 and 60°C, while the optimum for thermophilic fungi, that perform a similar role, is 40–50°C, which is also the optimum temperature for lignin degradation in compost. This is important as lignin found in leaves is generally resistant to decomposition. This makes green leaves slow to compost, often taking up to two years to decompose.

Like fungi, actinomycetes form threads, filaments or strands, which spread throughout a compost heap or soil. After bacteria, they are the second most abundant microorganism in a heap, with typically 100,000 to 100 million present in a gram of compost. They do not respond well to acidic conditions (below pH 5.5) or in the presence of a high moisture content.

Table 3.3 Aerobic composting vs anaerobic digestion

Aerobic	Anaerobic
Require little or no oxygen	Does not require, or in the absence of, oxygen
Rapid decomposition	Slower decomposition
Produces heat (most noticeable in larger bins)	Generates little heat
Hot compost can kill pathogens, seeds and weeds	Insufficient heat to kill weeds or pathogens
No pungent gas produced	Pungent gas produced e.g., hydrogen sulphide
Carbon dioxide is main gas released	Majority of energy released as methane
Produces compost	Produces sludge (digestate), which requires aerobic composting to complete process

Fungi

Fungi are active during the mesophilic and thermophilic phases of composting and break down cellulose and organic residues, enabling bacteria to proceed with the decomposition process.

Protozoa and Rotifers

Protozoa are single-celled microscopic animals, while rotifers are multicellular. They live in the water droplets around the organic particles. They have only a small role in the decomposition process, eating organic matter and, as secondary consumers, ingesting bacteria and fungi.

Aerobic and Anaerobic Respiration in Microorganisms

Microorganisms can be divided into those that respire aerobically, using the oxygen present in the air for energy metabolism, and anaerobic bacteria, which do not utilise oxygen for energy metabolism.

Conventional home and garden composting makes use of aerobic bacteria to produce compost from the organic waste. This requires the presence of certain factors, including air and moisture, and produces heat. Systems such as bokashi involve anaerobic decomposition. As the material is sealed in a container without air, it does not produce heat. A similar situation can occur if food waste is stored in a kitchen caddy or bin for more than a week or so. It will start to turn soft, mushy and eventually liquid, making it unpleasant to handle.

Although people may refer to the effects of anaerobic decomposition as 'composting', the precise definition of composting applies to aerobic decomposition only; the anaerobic process is actually digestion or fermentation.

Aerobic Bacteria

Aerobic bacteria are the most important microorganisms in the process of converting organic waste to compost. Vital for its conversion into a moist, rich end product, they require oxygen levels of more than 5% to oxidise carbon to provide them with energy. This oxidation process produces the heat that raises the temperature of the compost heap or bin during the early stages of the composting process. Under the right conditions, the compost will heat up within a day or two to 60°C or higher (*see* Chapter 4, on hot composting), due to the aerobic bacteria consuming the readily decomposable material.

In addition to carbon, nitrogen is also necessary to the composting process, enabling the bacteria to form the protein necessary for them to grow and reproduce. This is why it is important to be aware of the C:N ratio.

If the oxygen level falls below 5%, bacterial activity will slow down and the decomposition rate can be reduced by as much as 90%.

Anaerobic Bacteria

Where there is insufficient oxygen present to support the growth of aerobic microorganisms – in other words, the conditions are anaerobic – anaerobic bacteria will ferment the organic material. Unfortunately for the composter, the anaerobic process results in the production of organic acids and amines, producing the easily recognisable smell of ammonia, as well as hydrogen sulphide (which smells of rotten eggs). The organic material is turned into a wet, smelly black mess. In practice, if this happens it is because the C:N ratio is wrong. The situation may be rectified by adding more carbon-rich material (browns) and turning the compost to open the mix. This activity may be enough to create the conditions under which aerobic bacteria can function.

The requirement for a sufficiently moist mix during the composting process – ideally, 50–60% moisture content – is because the compost microorganisms live in the water films surrounding the particles of organic matter.

Bacterial Activity and Temperature

Composting is a self-heating, aerobic biodegradative process of organic materials. The microbes involved in the composting process perform best in the ideal conditions, but they will still do adequately well as long as the key requirements are in place:

- ventilation, to provide oxygen for their aerobic respiration;
- moisture, ideally 40–60%; and
- nutrients to support their growth.

When the microbes flourish, they will raise the heap temperature because of their metabolic heat generation during the conversion of composting materials to energy, carbon dioxide, water and compost. At different stages of the process, the temperature of the organic material and its nutrient content will vary, providing a favourable habitat for different types of microorganisms. Microorganisms can be grouped by the temperatures at which they can live.

The four stages of composting – initial, active, curing and maturing – can be classified by the temperatures created by the predominant bacteria groups at any time in the process. They have also been identified in terms of what is happening to the organic material in the Degradation, Conversion and Maturation (DCM) Classification. Technically, the stages are actually based on the activity of the different groups of organisms involved:

1. Psychrophilic or mesophilic stage: this is mainly a resting stage. It is not recognised as the first stage of the composting process by all, but it is important in colder climates. During this initial stage, mesophilic organisms predominate. It also represents the start of the degradation stage.
2. Active or thermophilic phase: this stage continues the degradation of the material. It may involve overheating if the process is not managed, with cooling as the food supply is exhausted, which may lead to a return to the mesophilic phase.
3. Maturation or cooling and curing phases: at this stage, the returning mesophilic organisms predominate.

More detailed technical knowledge on the microbiological stages of composting is not required when cold composting, which is the entry-level method and the technique used by most composters in the UK. However, it may be helpful for the composter who seeks a wider understanding of the practice, and it is essential when hot composting. For more on this technique, see Chapter 4 and, for the practical implications, Chapter 7.

The A, B and C of Cold Composting Materials

A: Chop into small pieces to increase surface area and speed up breakdown.
B: Mix nitrogen-rich greens and carbon-rich browns before or when adding to the bin.
C: Keep moist, adding water in hot dry weather.

PHASES OF HOT COMPOSTING: MICROORGANISMS, MACROORGANISMS AND PATHOGENS

In basic terms, then, composting is the natural process by which complex organic material such as food and plant waste are converted by aerobic biological decomposition to a dark humus-like substance. This process depends on certain conditions and the presence of composting creatures that play a vital role as first-, second- and third-level decomposers. Moving on from the basics, in traditional hot-composting systems microbial activity within the compost pile is optimised to produce temperatures of over 40–60°C. At this level, pathogens, weeds and seeds are killed and compost can be produced in a matter of weeks rather than months. Such systems were traditionally commonly used in larger gardens and on country estates, and examples can still be seen in practice by the public at many National Trust properties. In the past, of course, they would have been worked on by a team of full-time gardeners, but today the Trust relies on a huge group of volunteers to keep these environmentally friendly operations going.

Although most home composters will use a cold-composting system, they will still find it useful to have some knowledge of the techniques of hot composting. It will help with understanding the composting

When visiting a garden, it is worth checking out whether the composting area is open to the public.

process generally and provide relevant guidance when cold composting.

A composter using hot composting will usually have a three- or four-bin batch system, filling each bin at the same time, or at most within a couple of days. The different stages of the process are then managed with a view to maintaining the temperature in the thermophilic range for as long as practicable, in order to accelerate the composting process and to kill the pathogens. For more information on the practical aspects of traditional hot composting, *see* Chapter 7.

Hot composting in a bank of three bins involves turning the contents along the line, in order to aerate it and maintain the temperature.

A bank of pallet bins allows more flexibility in turning material to maintain thermophilic temperature.

Table 4.1 Phases of composting based on the temperature ranges of the microbes involved

Organisms involved	Temp range	Activity	Comment
Psychrophilic	-10–20°C	Most organisms are semi-dormant below 13°C, becoming more active as ambient temperature rises.	Degradation starts at about 12°C
Mesophilic	20–40°C	Active aerobic bacteria grow and reproduce producing heat, raising the temperature of the compost mass up to 40–45°C	When hot composting this stage will last 2 to 3 days
Thermophilic	40–70°C	Temperature rise occurs quickly. Depending on the materials, bin size and conditions, this phase may last a few days or can continue for weeks. When batch composting, all material should achieve this temperature range. Where fresh material is being added several times a week, the hotter temperatures will occur in the upper portion of the bin. In cold composting, hot spots are likely to be cooler and localised.	Active stage
Mesophilic	40–29°C	Cooling and curing or maturation. After the easily degradable materials have been utilised, actinomycetes, fungi and other microbes digest the more resistant materials. The temperature falls, allowing macroorganisms such as worms and woodlice to break down other organic materials.	Prolonged curing (up to 12 months) will reduce the risk of pathogens surviving

Psychrophilic Phase

Psychrophilic microorganisms function at low temperatures – from -10°C to +20°C (figures vary according to the source) – but below about 13°C most of the microorganisms in the heap will be semi-dormant and little decomposition of the organic material will occur. During the winter, the compost heap may become frozen and, even on warmer days, the temperature may not rise above 13°C.

At about 15°C, the psychrophiles become more active. They produce only a small amount of heat compared with other bacteria and can be active during the cold winter weather without significantly raising the temperature of the compost. As the weather becomes warmer, the heat they produce can be suffi-cient to increase the temperature of the heap or bin. As the temperature rises, the psychrophiles are dena-tured. At this point, a group of organisms that function at over 25°C, the mesophiles, become important to the process. Using the Degradation, Conversion and Maturation (DCM) classification, the degradation phase commences at about 12°C.

Mesophilic or Initial Phase

Many composters consider the mesophilic phase to be the first phase of real composting. This is a continua-tion of the degradation phase (under the DCM

classification). Mesophiles are found in water and soil and, under favourable conditions, they can double their numbers in 20 to 30 minutes. They are responsi-ble for most of the bacterial diseases in humans.

Mesophilic stage 28°C – the temperature (ambient) immediately after filling the bin.

Twenty-four hours after filling, the bin passes from the mesophilic to the thermophilic stage (about 40°C).

The phases of composting: microbial activity, turning and time. The dips in the thermophilic stage occur after turning the compost. Some people turn to aerate every two days, but turning weekly is acceptable.

When the compost is comfortably in the thermophilic range (40–70°C), seeds and pathogens will be killed. Turning and aerating the contents will prolong the time that the bin stays at these temperatures.

When a heap or pile is first made, the material is exposed to additional microorganisms and the microbes receive a fresh source of foodstuffs. The temperature and the presence of easily decomposed organic material favour the mesophilic bacteria and fungi, which quickly begin the decomposition of the easily digested materials in earnest, utilising soluble sugars and starch, until the heat produced by their activity causes the temperature of the heap to rise. Along with the heat, their activity also produces acids and carbon dioxide, causing a further rise in temperature. This moderate temperature mesophilic stage ranges between 20–40°C or as high as 45°C, although many mesophile species thrive best between 21°C and 32°C.

The initial mesophilic stage normally lasts for two or three days, with the organisms breaking down the soluble, more easily degraded organic compounds. As the temperature rises, thermophilic organisms begin to dominate.

In a cold-composting 'add as you go' system – for example, a small compost bin or heap – where organic material is added regularly in small amounts, the compost may never reach a higher temperature as the heat produced by bacterial activity is lost to the environment. The result of this is that the thermophiles do not become dominant and the mesophiles are left to do most of the work. This means that composting worms, which prefer temperatures of 20–25°C, should be active throughout the process.

During the mesophilic and thermophilic stages of the composting process, actinomycetes and fungi are confined to the outer 5–15cm (2–6in) of the heap or bin. Some moulds also grow in this outer zone of the composting galaxy. Unless the compost is aerated by frequent turning, the hyphae of fungi and actinomycetes can give a grey or white appearance to this outer zone. Turning the cooler material of the outer areas into the centre of the heap prevents the formation of sufficient hyphae to produce a colour change that is visible to the naked eye.

Thermophilic or 'Active' Phase

The activity of the mesophiles results in the production of heat and a significant increase in the temperature of the heap (40 to 70°C) so that it begins to favour thermophilic organisms. These are the most efficient decomposing bacteria in a hot-composting pile and continue the degradation phase (under the DCM classification). They start to dominate the heap at temperatures of about 40°C and composting proceeds at a much faster rate under thermophilic conditions. It is during this stage that most of the organic matter is converted into carbon dioxide and humus. There is also a growth in the number of microorganisms present.

The high temperatures accelerate the breakdown of cellulose, hemicellulose and other complex carbohydrates, proteins and fats. The thermophilic population continues generating more heat by decomposing the remaining organic matter. As this food source is utilised, the activity of the thermophilic microbes declines. Unless the heap is regularly fed new material and turned, to move materials from the cool sides to the centre, the temperature of the compost will fall after three to 12 days (depending on the technique being used). This allows the return of mesophilic organisms, which once again become the dominant group of bacteria in the compost heap. During this period, the conversion phase (DCM classification) begins. In a compost bin or heap, the conversion will occur at the bottom, as the organic material starts to take on the appearance of compost.

The period of thermophilic activity can be extended by turning the heap and aeration, and some composters will turn the material as often as weekly or even twice-weekly for the first month. The Berkeley rapid composting technique developed at the University of California involves turning at two-day intervals and should be operated at 55–65°C for 18 days (see Chapter 7). Other methods involving regular turning can produce compost in six weeks or less, depending on the frequency of turning.

Alternatively, the turning can be undertaken based on the temperature of the heap. If it falls below 50°C or 55°C, it can be turned in order to aerate, mix and increase microbial activity. Temperature measurement followed by turning when required is continued until there is no marked change in temperature following the aeration.

The killing of pathogens, weeds and seeds is one advantage of hot-composting techniques, but it is not necessary unless there is a specific concern about diseased organisms or about weed seeds surviving.

Compost near the top of the desired range. It should be turned if the temperature reaches 72°C.

When cold composting it is advisable not to add diseased materials to the bin in the first place. Germinating weed seeds that survive cold composting can be attacked with a hoe.

Many 'good' bacteria (in other words, decomposers) are inactivated or killed when the temperature of the heap rises above 60°C (140°F). If the heap temperature exceeds 72°C (160°F), it can be cooled by turning/aerating. If a pile does overheat, exceeding 76°C, many of the bacteria will be destroyed and the composting process will come almost to a stop. It has been found that during the thermophilic stage in some bins, 87% of the organisms present were *bacillus* species. These are spore-forming, with one species (*Bacillus stearothermophilus*) predominant at temperatures of over 65°C. Spores are formed by bacteria of the species *bacillus* and *clostridium* as a survival mechanism when the organism is under stress such as heat. The spores will survive the difficult conditions and will go on to germinate once the heap has cooled to a more suitable temperature.

Fungi such as *Rhizomucor pusillus* (*Mucor pusillus*) are also active as the temperature rises – *R. pusillus* has an optimum temperature range of 50–70°C – but are inactivated at the highest temperatures. A second group of thermophilic fungi play a role in the decomposition of cellulose and hemicelluloses, including *Aspergillus fumigatus*, a potential human pathogen.

Eventually, insufficient nutrients will be available to maintain the higher temperatures and the heap will return to the cooler levels of the mesophilic stage, even when turned.

There is another traditional approach to hot composting, which involves batch-filling a large, layered bin – a 2.5-m (8-ft) version has been used in some gardens – and leaving it for several months. Layered and batch-filled 1-m (3-ft) bins may also be used, with very little weed growth resulting. In cold composting, most of the heap will not exceed 40°C. Although thermophilic temperatures may be reached briefly in some parts of a cold-composting heap, especially after new material is added, it is mesophiles not thermophiles that will do most of the work.

Mesophilic, Curing or Maturation Phase

At this stage of the composting process, the easily degradable organic materials will have been utilised. The material that is left is insoluble in water and cannot be absorbed into the bacterial cells due to their chemical complexity and size. The fungi and actinomycetes now dominate as they degrade these compounds using extracellular enzymes, allowing them to be absorbed. The materials include chitin, lignins, humic materials, some remaining cellulose, starches and proteins. As they are reduced, carbon, nitrogen and ammonia are liberated, making nutrients available for higher plants. They are especially important in the formation of humus – organic matter that has reached the final state of decomposition – and are responsible

Compost matured in a pallet bin. Fungi and actinomycetes play a major role in this stage. It has been covered during maturation.

for the earthy smell associated with compost. They usually appear five to seven days after the start of the composting process. Actinomycetes develop into large clusters and become most evident during the later stages of decomposition.

Actinomycetes assume a major role during the final stages of decomposition and may produce antibiotics that inhibit bacterial growth. They work on organic materials that are tough to break down, such as avocado, seeds and glossy leaves. To avoid breaking up the hyphae of actinobacteria (and fungi), turning tumbler composters during the curing phase is not recommended, and compost in conventional heaps, piles or bins should not be mixed or aerated.

Fungi also play a significant role during the final stages of composting. Fungi are primitive plants that can be either single-celled or many-celled and filamentous. They are present in smaller numbers in the compost than actinomycetes or bacteria, but are larger in body mass. Their main contribution to a compost pile is to break down cellulose and lignin. They prefer cooler temperatures of 22–24°C and easily digested food sources.

During the curing and maturation stage of composting, the cooler temperatures encourage the entry of worms, insects, mites and the other microorganisms.

The time of the curing process will vary but a longer process is desirable as it reduces the likelihood of pathogens and phytotoxins being present, as well as organic acids, which may limit the use of the end product as seed compost. The levels of humus in the compost also increase with the length of the curing process.

Maturation in an open bin. The active composting process has been completed and the compost left to over-winter in the bay. Stinging-nettle growth will often occur in open bays during maturation.

Growth of actinomycetes in compost.

In home composting any available bin can be used to mature the compost. Alternatively, specially designed maturation bins can be purchased.

Cold or Hot Composting?

While enthusiasts tend to use active hot-composting techniques, new entrants and many householders use a cool or cold passive-composting set-up, as it is simpler and requires less hands-on time and effort. The organic material from the kitchen and garden is added to the bin as and when it becomes available, and the contents of the bin or heap are probably not mixed regularly. The disadvantage of this technique is that it is slow, taking six to 18 months.

During cold composting there is insufficient microbial activity for the bin contents to reach temperatures at which the organic material can decompose quickly, or potential pathogens and seeds can be killed. Inevitably, there are considerable variations in temperature within a bin or heap, and between different bins and heaps, as the feedstock is added at different times and in different proportions.

Microbial activity within the bin will normally generate sufficient metabolic heat to keep the temperature above the ambient air temperature. However, during the winter the compost temperature will usually be below 15°C and in cold periods may fall into psychrophilic range (5–10°C). It can be expected to be in the mesophilic range (15–45°C) from late spring and in early summer. In the middle of summer, when temperatures are high and there are plenty of soft greens

Cold composting on an allotment.

in the feedstock, the temperature may even reach the thermophilic range of over 40°C.

Compost Microorganisms that are Pathogenic to Humans

There are many disease-causing microorganisms that may be found as contaminants of compost and could present a risk of infection to the composter. These include the food-poisoning bacteria that are often featured in the press following an outbreak of disease – *salmonella, campylobacter, Clostridia perfringens, E. coli, Staphylococcus aureus* – as well as other pathogens such as *Clostridia tetani* and *Coxiella burnettii* (the cause of Q fever), *erysipelothrix, leptospira, listeria, pasteurella* and *mycobacterium*.

The risk from material from a private kitchen or garden is relatively low as it is less likely to be contaminated with animal and faecal waste than materials collected by kerb-side collection or from other sources. Luckily, most of the pathogenic bacteria, if present, will not be in large enough numbers to cause disease in humans. In most cases, the hot-composting process, and time, will kill those that remain.

Bioaerosols (airborne microorganisms, including bacteria and fungi spores) have been implicated in incidences of infection in industrial composting plants and there have been some rare cases associated with home composting. The number of bioaerosols will be dependent on the degree of contamination of the initial organic material, the growth of the organisms while awaiting composting, multiplication during the composting process and the actual activity being undertaken. Activities that pose a higher risk to the composter or gardener include turning and sieving compost and any process that involves disturbing compost on which mould is growing or that smells mouldy. For basic safety precautions, *see* Chapter 1.

CHAPTER 5

ENTRY-LEVEL COMPOSTING

It is said that 'compost just happens', but there are ways and means of helping it to happen, with minimum cost and effort. Evidence suggests that new composters are easily put off when they encounter problems and may stop composting as a result. To try to avoid this happening, this chapter will suggest entry-level cold-composting systems using the basic bins that are available to all new composters and require the least effort, knowledge and cost. The advice will be most useful to first-time composters or those who do not want to invest much time and effort, but hopefully the results achieved will encourage everyone to increase their knowledge and progress to more advanced techniques.

Even cheaper than the basic bins, but less popular in the UK, are the traditional heap, sheet and trench compost systems, and leaf mould manufacture.

Choosing a Bin

Plastic Bins

Although trench and sheet composting methods require no expenditure or equipment, they are used by a relatively small number of composters. Most people in the UK start composting using cold (or passive)

composting techniques and purchasing a basic moulded plastic compost bin, sometimes under a discount scheme offered by their local council. There are a few advantages of using a lidded plastic compost bin rather than the traditional heap: it contains the compost; it excludes rainwater, reducing leachate soaking into the ground; and it helps keep vermin out of the compost. In addition, if the bin is not too heavy or has a large hatch, it is easy to harvest the finished compost from it. The use of a bin rather than a heap also keeps the garden looking tidier.

There is a wide variety of entry-level cone- or 'Dalek'-shaped moulded or sectional plastic bins (see

Entry-level bins on allotment plots.

'Dalek'-style bins are often supplied under council discount schemes.

A more expensive bin, with a hatch and aeration slots.

Chapter 2) available. They come in a range of sizes and prices, but there is an argument to be made in favour of gaining initial experience of composting using low-cost equipment. In this way, a more informed choice can be made when committing to any more significant expenditure. Even a low-cost bin provides an excellent

entry to composting for busy people looking for a 'lazy' approach, requiring minimum time and effort. On larger vegetable plots, the 220-litre or 330-litre bins available through the discount schemes may not be big enough to cope with all the material produced. However, if composting with a single bin is successful, additional similar bins may be purchased, or the use of larger, more expensive plastic, wooden or home-made pallet bins may be considered.

The basic moulded bins can be divided into two groups: those with a hatch that allows compost to be harvested without moving the bin, and those without a hatch.

The entry-level bins that have a hatch positioned at the bottom are designed to allow the finished compost to be harvested without disturbing the recently added material at the top. There are three types of hatch. The type fitted to the 'Dalek' bins (generally the style of bin that is supplied under council discount schemes) clips into place while the hatch on the slightly more expensive bins can be slid open. On both types, the opening tends to be rather small, making it difficult to fully remove the compost. Most people end up lifting the bin off the contents, leaving it in a heap with the finished compost at the bottom and the uncomposted material at the top. The hatch is still useful, though, as it can be removed to check whether the material in the bin is ready to harvest.

The third type of hatch is to be found on many of the mid-range sectional bins (see Chapter 6), where one of the rods holding the sections in place is partially withdrawn, allowing the lower section to be swung open.

A single moulded bin may be sufficient for a small garden. More can be added as required.

An example of a sliding hatch cover.

Recognising the problems associated with removing waste through a hatch, some manufacturers have done away with them and have designed their bins in the shape of a cone, making it easier to lift the bin off the pile. There are also 'straight'-sided bins available. Lifting the bin off the compost may be beyond the capabilities of some gardeners. If this is the case, the bin can be pushed over and then lifted or rolled away from the compost.

Moulded plastic Rotol bins without hatches. The shape of these bins makes it easier to lift the bin off the compost to harvest the contents.

Some types of hatch cover push into place.

Clip-in hatches may distort in use.

Straight-sided bin without a hatch.

Compost can be harvested from a bin without a hatch by lifting the bin off the compost or pushing it over.

A small single-chamber entry-level tumbler bin that has a larger capacity than the dual-chamber models.

Plastic bins are also available at entry-level prices in the form of small tumblers with single and double bins. They are usually too small for hot composting, but they do provide an easy way of aerating small amounts of cold compost.

Wooden Bins

Slatted wooden bins with removable front slats, which make it easy to access and turn the composting materials, are popular among new composters who want their garden to have a traditional look. The bins can be lined with cardboard or plastic to retain heat. On allotments and larger gardens, wooden pallet bins may be the entry level equipment of choice as the pallets are often available free of charge.

Wooden bins with solid sides offer an alternative to those with slatted sides, but they tend to be slightly more expensive.

Filling the bin in distinct layers, to achieve the correct green:brown ratio, is easier with a conventional square wooden bin than with a plastic moulded type. Because of this, wooden bins are a good choice to develop layering techniques if there is a likelihood of progressing to larger-scale composting. If the system is later upgraded to mid- or higher-level bins, the initial bin can be usefully repurposed as a maturation bin in which compost that is almost finished can complete the composting process.

This dual-chamber tumbler bin is probably too small for hot composting but does provide a means of treating limited amounts of waste.

Entry-level slatted wooden compost bin. The front slats can be easily removed when turning the waste.

Other containers such as this plastic crate may be used as a bin.

Plastic pallets being used in a bank of three. An entry-level pallet bin can easily be expanded for use by an enthusiast.

A bin made with the pallets laid so that the slats are vertical.

Bins Made from Other Materials

Enterprising allotment-holders will often build a compost bin from whatever materials are to hand at the time. Concrete slabs and bricks are quite commonly seen on allotments – they may be cemented to form a permanent structure, or loose stacked and removed as the compost is harvested. Metal sheeting and weldmesh may also be put to good use. Builders' bags can be usefully repurposed as temporary compost bins; they should last another year or two before their eventual disposal.

Old tyres are occasionally used to make temporary bins. They are cheap but not very practical, as all the tyres have to be lifted to retrieve compost from the

A home-made wooded bin. lined with plastic to help insulate the contents.

Entry-level bins can also be made of concrete blocks or brick, which may be cemented or left loose, as in this case, allowing the bin to be modified.

Metal sheeting is often used to make a bin. In this case, the sheeting appears to have been a curved shed roof originally.

Builders' bags can be used as temporary compost bins; if the bottom is removed, the bag can be lifted off the compost for harvesting.

bottom. Many allotments ban tyres from the site because of disposal problems.

There was a time when asbestos was used on allotments to construct sheds and compost bins. The use of this dangerous material on allotments is now banned but that does not mean that it is not sometimes introduced without permission or found on a long-established plot....

Different materials and designs may lend a certain charm to an allotment site, and it will be a sorry day

A simple bin of wire netting.

A bin made of netting on a pallet base.

A bin made from tyres, which must be lifted to retrieve compost from the bottom of the bin. The rubber may degrade with time and eventual disposal will cost money.

If identified, asbestos bins should be removed and disposed of in accordance with the regulations.

Asbestos cement sheet being used as bin front.

A gardener taking on an allotment should not be put off if there is a pallet bin on the plot that shows signs of disrepair. The pallets can be replaced and the compost used.

that any committee or landlord tries to standardise the construction of compost bins. However, not all structures are well maintained and not all allotments are well managed. Those starting to compost should not be put off by the poor techniques of others.

Locating the Bin or Heap

A correctly operated compost bin or heap should not smell bad, but during the learning process there may be occasions when things go wrong, resulting in an unpleasant odour and on occasions an abundance of fruit flies. The general advice, therefore, is not to locate the bin too close to the house because of any possible smells but still as close as practicable, to avoid frequent trips down the garden. A kitchen caddy can solve the problem of having to visit the bin every day, but it is nonetheless advisable to site it as close as possible to the part of the garden where most of the waste will be produced.

In a small garden with a single bin, a compost storage area may not be needed. In a larger garden, storage and access space will be required around the bin or bins, to allow the contents to be turned and the bin emptied. Where batch composting is being considered, additional space may be required for the compostable material to be separated into browns and greens until there is enough compostable waste to fill, or almost fill, the bin in one go.

Most bins benefit from a sunny location, but this may not be the case in a hotter climate, where the bin might be dried out regularly. Finally, when installing a bin, it is important to avoid creating a rat run by placing it too close to a wall or solid fence.

As people become more enthusiastic, they often progress to more or bigger bins.

Materials for composting

Materials that *can* be composted

Greens

- Uncooked fruit and vegetable peelings, leaves and plants
- Grass cuttings
- Weeds (roots of perennial weeds should be drowned or dried first)
- Soft green prunings
- Cut flowers and bedding plants
- Nettle and comfrey leaves
- Coffee grounds, tea leaves and bags
- Droppings from any healthy vegetarian pets and chickens
- Manure from herbivores, for example, cows and horses
- Urine (ideally diluted 20:1)

Hot Composted

- Cooked food waste, meat and fish, bones (in an enclosed rat-proof bin)
- Diseased plants

Browns

- Bedding (hay, shredded paper, straw, wood shavings) from vegetarian pets and chickens
- Cardboard (for example, boxes, cereal packets, egg boxes, kitchen and toilet roll tubes)

- Waste paper and junk mail, including shredded confidential documents
- Paper towels
- Woody prunings and hedge clippings (shredded)
- Old bedding plants
- Hay and straw
- Paper, scrunched up or shredded
- Autumn leaves

Also compostable

- Wood ash (small amounts)
- Hair (including pet hair)
- Nail clippings
- Eggshells
- Natural fibres (for example wool and cotton)

Material that *cannot* be composted

- Coal and coke ash
- Cat litter
- Human poo
- Disposable nappies
- Dog poo (may be composted safely if controls are in place to limit worm infestation of the dog, and measures are taken to avoid human contact, by maintaining separation from other waste and food crops when the compost is used)

Materials for Composting

Garden Waste

Garden waste includes grass cuttings, trimmed leaves from vegetables, annual and perennial weeds, autumn leaves, twigs, old patio plants and finished vegetable plants. All can be chopped to about 5–15cm (2–6in) in length using garden shears if necessary and added straight to the bin. Bedding from vegetarian pets and chicken can also be added. Sawdust and woodchip can be composted and are often used as a bulking agent when composting cooked food.

Kitchen Waste

Collection of kitchen waste may require a degree of separation depending on the types of waste and the composting techniques to be used. Initial separation is normally into uncooked and cooked food waste as the cooked food will smell and produce liquid when left in a caddy for more than a day or two.

To avoid smells in the kitchen and too many trips down the garden to the compost bin, it is advisable to use a kitchen caddy with an airtight lid to collect the waste from day to day. One way of doing this is to have a set of two 5-litre caddies, one for uncooked kitchen waste, for the wormeries, and a second for onion, garlic, citrus and cooked food, which is composted. The onion and garlic are put into this second caddy partly to avoid odours in the house. It is also because some sources advise that onion and garlic and acidic citrus pulp should be added to wormeries only in small quantities or even excluded completely. The cooked food and onion/garlic/citrus waste is taken directly to the cooked-food compost bin or added directly to a bokashi bin. (Bokashi is a fermentation system that converts food waste, including cooked food, to a pre-compost that can then be added to a conventional cold-composting bin or buried in the garden; *see* Chapter 11 for more on this.)

Coffee grounds are a good green from the kitchen and can give the bin a boost during the winter months. Used grounds may also be collected from many cafés for free.

Eggshells from the kitchen can also be composted. Some people take the trouble to wash them but most either put them in the caddy as they are or crush them and then put them in. Some even grind them with a pestle and mortar.

It is not necessary to use a commercially available caddy – any recycled container or lidded bucket can be used – but there is a wide range of plastic, pottery or metal versions designed for the collection of kitchen waste. A solid-sided plastic caddy with an airtight lid can be easily cleaned, and many are dishwasher proof. Some are quite large, but it is best to use one that will be filled in a couple of days, to avoid unpleasant smells. A layer of newspaper in the bottom of the caddy will absorb some of the moisture from the food, making it easier to tip the waste into the bin.

Some kitchen caddies include a charcoal filter to reduce any potential smells, but this will need to be easy to remove when washing the caddy. Others have ventilation holes in the sides, but these require the addition of a compostable paper or corn-starch bag, which can then be lifted out and added straight to the compost bin. These are really designed for use with kerbside food waste collection services such as those operated by local councils. In this case, the council may provide a caddy for use in the kitchen, along with a larger container that is kept outside and collected as part of the kerbside collection. A ventilated caddy allows evaporation, reducing the weight of the waste to be collected. If cooked food is not being home composted, this type provides an excellent means of dealing with food waste.

A range of kitchen caddies and a food waste kerbside bin (back row, centre). The one in the front centre is metal, while all the others are plastic and may be machine washed.

Coffee waste collected daily in kitchen caddies from a small café. Many cafes will bag and give their coffee grounds to composters.

Other Household Waste

Much of the garden and kitchen waste is made up of materials that are known in composting terms as greens. An effective working bin will need a balance between greens and browns. Luckily, the average household generates a good supply of browns in the form of cardboard, paper, egg boxes, the inner tubes from toilet and kitchen rolls, and the wood-based bedding from vegetarian pets.

Meat and dairy products, coal ash, dog and cat faeces, fish and bones, fats, grease or oils should not be composted using a basic compost bin.

Using an Entry-Level Compost Bin

A good airflow is required within the bin to ensure aerobic composting, so a layer of twigs, or a seasonal equivalent such as brassica or Jerusalem artichoke stalks, should be put in the bottom 15cm (6in) of a bin that is placed directly on the soil. If using a plastic bin with a hatch, care should be taken not to use sticks that are too thick. Any wood that remains undecomposed will make it difficult to remove the finished compost via the hatch using a spade. Any coarse brown material, such as woodchip, straw, corrugated cardboard (which is excellent, as it traps the air) or scrunched-up cardboard boxes, can be used instead.

Ideally, garden waste should be cut into short lengths before being added to the bin or heap. Long-handled shears will save the composter's back.

Adding Waste

The process of decomposition is accelerated if the garden and kitchen waste is cut into small pieces before being put in the bin (*see* Chapter 3). The fresh material being added should be roughly equal parts greens and browns – in a square bin, it is easy to make layers 10–15cm (4–6in) thick, while waste can be added to a plastic cold-composting bin as and when the caddy is full. Ideally, each caddy of greens should be matched with approximately the same volume of browns. Adjustments to the mix can be made by eye: if it is too dry, more greens are added; if it is too wet, browns are added. In the case of a wooden bin, it is easier to add the greens and browns to make separate layers as materials become available.

Stalks are best cut to less than 5cm (2in) but in practice longer pieces can be used, particularly if they are crushed with a hammer (*see* Chapter 3).

Uncooked fruit and vegetable waste, including coffee filters, can be added directly from the kitchen caddy to the compost bin or wormery.

When adding browns, such as cardboard and paper, it is best to shred or tear them into small pieces. The correct moisture level may be maintained by sprinkling each layer or addition of browns with water. The ingredients need to stay moist for decomposition to occur – the objective is to maintain a moisture level similar to that of a wrung-out sponge.

Autumn leaves can also be added as a brown. When being added to an entry-level bin they are best mixed well with greens, such as grass. It is advisable to aerate the upper layers of a non-layered bin when fresh material is added, to mix the greens and browns in the upper active layers. A garden or manure fork can be used to turn the contents in a square wooden bin, but a special compost aeration tool may be easier to use in a conical bin (*see* Chapter 3).

Cardboard as a brown layer in a bin. It is best torn or shredded.

Cardboard is easier to tear when it is wet, so there is an added advantage to using it as a temporary cover until it rains.

Shredded autumn leaves can also be added as a brown.

Woodchip is a useful brown and a good bulking agent when food composting. It is best part-composted and then allowed to dry before use.

To keep the number of flies and other insects to a minimum, browns can be added to form a top layer in the bin. Shredded paper is often used at home with lidded bins while a layer of soil or woodchip can be used on the allotment and when the contents are not going to be turned. The compost should be covered but will need watering to keep the contents moist, while soil or woodchip is probably better on an open-topped bin.

During decomposition, the contents of the bin will shrink. Without the addition of more material, the finished compost will be reduced to between one-quarter and one-third of its original size.

Shredded computer and wrapping paper provide easily mixed browns.

Harvesting the Compost

If the contents of a bin are not turned regularly, composting can take between six and 18 months, after which a significant proportion will have been converted to compost, working from the bottom up. When materials are added to the bin in small quantities as they become available, the top layers will not be composted unless the contents have been mixed regularly and then left for some time without any further additions. If the bin has a hatch, the finished compost can be removed through it. However, if the hatch is small, this can be rather laborious. If the bin does not have a base, it may be easier to lift it off the compost, although this may leave a pile that looks like an untidy Christmas pudding!

One of the factors to consider when choosing a bin is the ease of harvesting the compost. For example, lifting the bin off the compost is easier with a conical bin such as the Rotol, and a wooden bin with a removable front or a sectional plastic mid-range bin with a large opening at the base will allow easier removal of the finished material.

Where more than one entry-level bin is being used, many composters will not treat transfer material between the bins, as in a hot-composting system used by more experienced enthusiasts. Instead, they will fill each bin separately before moving to the next.

To decide whether compost is ready to be removed from a bin, a simple maturity test can be performed by sealing a sample of the compost in a bag and leaving it for three days. If, when it is reopened, it has a pleasant earthy smell, composting has finished. On the other hand, if it smells unpleasant, the composting process has not been completed. For more information on home-testing compost, *see* Chapter 12.

Harvesting from a 'Dalek' bin using the hatch.

Entry-level bins on an allotment. They form only part of the composting on this particular plot.

The compost does not need to be moved between bins. Many people fill one bin and then move on to fill the next.

Compost bins with part of the garden: a reminder that composting is about growing and soil improvement.

If the process has not been completed, the uncomposted material can be returned to the bin, mixed well (aerated) and watered if it is dry. Some composters use this process of removing the bin, mixing the compost and returning it to the bin at regular intervals to aerate the contents and speed up the composting process.

Making Leaf Mould

Autumn leaves are an often-underrated free resource and the making of leaf mould is an entry-level technique. As well as being used for making leaf mould, autumn leaves can be kept dry and saved for adding as a 'brown' to a composting system during the winter months. They can also be used as a mulch, in a layer when lasagne composting, and as worm bedding.

Making leaf mould. Spreading autumn leaves on the lawn and then shredding them by mowing adds grass (a green) as part of the process. This is an alternative to using a shredder.

Part of the leaf mould corner at the Stokes Wood demonstration site, using bags, Geobin composters and a modified compost bin.

Leaves tend to be slow to decompose, but their breakdown can be accelerated by putting them through a leaf shredder or scattering them on the lawn and passing over them with a rotary lawnmower. When the grass from the lawn is mixed with the shredded leaves, their decomposition will be accelerated. The leaves of the more common UK trees, such as oak, beech and hornbeam, break down comparatively

Making leaf mould using a traditional leaf-mould bin of wire netting.

Making leaf mould using a plastic bag. The leaves are added to the bag, then watered. The bag is sealed, stabbed with a fork and left for two years.

Making leaf mould in a biodegradable sack; the sack itself may decompose more quickly than the leaves from some trees.

Leaf mould being made in a conventional compost bin.

easily to produce good-quality leaf mould, while horse and sweet chestnut and sycamore are slower to break down. Conifer needles are slower still. They should be treated separately, in any case, as they produce an acidic material, which is ideal for mulching ericaceous plants.

Traditionally, leaf mould was made by piling the leaves in a heap and keeping it sufficiently wet to prevent them blowing all over the garden. Alternatively, they can be imprisoned within a cage of wire netting, made simply by fixing chicken wire to four posts. The Geobin plastic mesh compost bin provides a tidier and long-lasting alternative to wire mesh and is easily adjustable in size. As with composting, larger bins work best, so the container should be at least 1 metre square. The bottom of the bin can be lined with weed suppressant or cardboard.

Both these methods work well, but leaf mould can be made more quickly and easily by filling plastic refuse sacks or old compost bags with leaves and compressing them. Grass can be included to speed decomposition and the mixture should be watered but not soaked. The bag is secured, stabbed several times with a garden fork, and then left in a corner of the garden for six to 12 months. It should be checked periodically to ensure that the contents are still wet.

Second-hand builders' bulk bags can also be used for making leaf mould. This type of bag is permeable, allowing excess moisture to drain away. Some people support the corners of the bag with stakes. The bag will be very heavy when filled so it might be advisable to cut the bottom out so that it can be lifted off the leaf

Leaf mould in two Geobins.

Making leaf mould in an open plastic bin.

mould when the decomposed leaves are ready for reuse. For best results, the bag should be checked during hot or dry periods to monitor the moisture content.

Leaf mould in the early stages.

Leaf mould after one year in a plastic sack.

Simple and Traditional Systems

There are a number of simple entry-level systems – for example, sheet, lasagne, trench and post-hole composting, grass boarding and Hügelkultur mound systems – that are easy to set up and in most cases involve little or no expense. For some reason, they are not as popular as the use of bins for composting, but there is certainly scope for all of them to be used more widely.

Sheet Composting

In sheet composting, organic material is simply spread over an area of the garden and composted in situ. It builds up organic soil content quickly and involves less work than using a heap or bin. The main advantage for gardeners with large gardens is that a substantial amount of material can be composted with minimum effort. Sheet composting provides a cheap way of filling a raised bed rather than using purchased commercial compost. A further advantage is that, if the soil conditions are right – airy, moist, warm and with high levels of nutrients – it will produce compost fairly quickly, provided the organic materials have the correct carbon:nitrogen ratio. If there is too much carbon, the soil will be depleted of nutrients during the initial stages of decay while the surplus carbon has been consumed. This is a common problem when woody material is spread on the garden.

It is best to prepare the area to be composted by removing any pernicious or persistent weeds or, if the area is mainly grass, by mowing or scalping it down to the lowest possible height. It also helps to loosen the soil underneath the proposed bed, to improve drainage. The area is then covered with four to six overlapping layers of newspaper or cardboard, as a carbon material that will smother the grass. The newspaper or cardboard is soaked thoroughly and covered with a 2.5cm (1in) layer of green garden waste. This might include fresh green annual weeds, comfrey, nettles or manure, or a mix of any of these. This is followed by a layer of browns, such as cardboard, leaves, shredded paper or straw.

Vermin may be a problem if food waste is used when sheet composting. They should be less of a problem if the waste is buried, as it is in trench composting, although some creatures may still be able to find it. The compost can take a long time to break down in this system, so there is a need to plan ahead for any future requirements for garden compost.

Grass Boarding

Grass boarding is a type of sheet composting that is very useful for a composter who has a large lawn or access to grassed areas that are regularly mown, such as the paths and car park on an allotment site, a small paddock or bowling green.

The cut grass is spread 2.5cm (1in) deep and covered by a layer of carboard or used paper towels (which may be available at a school or other workplace). Alternate layers of grass and cardboard are added until the heap reaches the desired height. Care should be taken not to compress the heap. This may result in anaerobic fermentation, which will result in a smelly mess. Dry straw or leaves may also be used and a little soil can be added between the layers.

The technique can be used on open ground, where the grass cuttings will form a heap. Alternatively, the material can be enclosed within a wooden frame or kept in a dedicated compost bin. In the compost bin variation of grass boarding, 20cm (8in) layers of grass clippings may be alternated with cardboard, crumpled paper or other browns, such as dried leaves. The brown layer can be covered with a thin 2.5cm (1in) layer of soil, to help absorb gases and water.

Lasagne Composting

The lasagne variation of sheet composting is popular with 'no-dig' gardeners and provides a low-cost means of filling a raised bed (see also Chapter 2). It involves an initial layer of wet corrugated cardboard, or three layers of newspaper, laid directly on top of the soil or grass. At its simplest, alternate layers of browns and greens are added, often to a height of about 60cm (2ft). The brown layers should be twice as deep as the green.

This excellent method of filling a raised bed is open to adaptation – one example is an initial layer of soaked cardboard followed by a thick layer of grass clippings followed by a layer of compost mixed with topsoil. The layers are then repeated as necessary.

Trench Composting

Trench composting (see also Chapter 2) is particularly useful in the vegetable garden and often used in the late summer and autumn prior to planting rows of beans or squashes the following spring. In fact, many gardeners consider using a trench filled with waste vegetable material as the normal method of preparing a bean row without thinking of it as a form of composting.

Trench composting provides a simple way for composting fruit and vegetable waste including uncooked kitchen scraps without the need for special equipment. Once the material has been buried, there is no visible evidence that composting is being undertaken. It also provides a way of dealing with bokashi pre-compost.

Decomposition in underground composting happens more slowly than in the more usual bin systems and, depending on the depth of the trench, the type of soil and the prevailing conditions, this system may involve anaerobic decomposition. For this reason, it is perhaps more important than in normal systems to expose the maximum surface area of the material to microbial activity, so cutting the waste to about 5cm (2in)

Trench composting: the material is covered with the soil removed when digging the trench.

in length is recommended. The greens and browns can be mixed in the trench using a fork or spade, but it is probably easier to mix them before adding to the trench.

When using trench composting to grow runner beans, it can be started at any time of year, but autumn is ideal, as the material will have decomposed and the site will be ready for planting in the spring. If there is space available on the plot, trench composting can be started earlier in the year. This will allow chopped brassica stalks to be included, which is useful, as this type of waste may be slow to compost in a conventional compost bin. Trenches can also be dug between rows of plants or seeds. The trench depth can vary from 45 to 60cm (18–24in) and it can be one or two spade widths wide. As the soil is removed, it is placed alongside the trench so that it may be used later to cover the vegetable waste as it is added, starting at one end. Some people dig a deeper trench so that a second layer of waste can be added. When the waste has been covered, it is likely to have created a mound along the length of the trench, but this will have settled down by the time of planting. It is advisable to mark the trench with small sticks so it can be easily located when it is ready to use.

Some gardeners use trench composting as part of a composting rotational system, moving the trench across the plot each year.

Post-Hole Composting

Post-hole composting deserves to be more popular than it is as it can be useful in a flower garden or a smaller vegetable garden, with the waste being added to discreet holes dug where there is exposed soil between plants. With planning, it will not be necessary to store the waste before burial and of course there is no compost to harvest as the waste decomposes in situ. Alternatively, individual holes can be dug where space allows in the garden.

Post-hole composting is a method that requires no special equipment or expenditure. At the simplest level, a spade or post-hole digger can be used to make a hole at least 30–45cm (12–18in) deep – deep enough so that the waste can be covered with at least 10cm (4in) of soil – with the width being varied to suit the volume of waste. If meat, dairy or cooked food are being buried in a trench, it needs to be deeper, with space for at least 30cm (12in) of soil on top. The waste material should be moistened before being covered. The soil can be covered with straw or other mulch to provide additional protection.

Hügelkultur Mound

In this permaculture technique, large pieces of rotting wood are buried so that they decompose in the ground while allowing the cultivation of plants on the raised mound, or, less commonly, a sunken bed. It may be considered as a combined raised bed and compost heap and is said to remain fertile for up to six years.

Composting and growing in mounds has been used in Eastern Europe for hundreds of years. It is an environmentally friendly means of disposing of logs and other unwanted woody material, including quite thick logs and tree stumps, as an alternative to bonfires. It also provides an interesting additional composting tool. It is not intended to replace the insect- and hedgehog-friendly wood pile in the garden, but a communal hügelkultur bed snaking its way across those areas where the ground is unsuitable for cultivation, or as a boundary to a car park, could become a feature of every allotment site.

The technique normally involves digging a trench, but the mound can also be built directly on the soil. Wet cardboard can be used in the bottom of the trench, or the wood can be laid directly on the soil. Logs, branches and other woody matter that decomposes slowly are placed in the bottom of the trench. The larger items are deposited first, with the smaller branches, twigs, leaves, woodchip and other compostable materials added over the top of the woody layer, ideally filling in the gaps between the larger pieces of wood. A discarded Christmas tree can be included in this layer. A bed can also be built around tree stumps, providing an alternative to removing them. It will help if the larger stumps and logs are already rotting and the addition of nitrogen-rich urine is said to be beneficial too.

As the technique normally involves building a raised bed that will be planted, rather than a traditional compost heap, the mound does not need to be hidden at the bottom of the garden but can be in view. This makes it easier to choose a site where it would be beneficial to have plants growing on the mound once it is established.

The simplest bed, which will be suitable for a smaller garden, can consist of small mounds about 60cm (2ft) high of rotting wood or sticks placed directly on forked-over ground and layered closely together. Grass clippings and other nitrogen-rich greens such as manure are then added, filling any gaps between the logs and sticks. The mound is then covered by 5cm (2in) of topsoil.

With larger mounds, a trench is desirable, as it helps keep the mound tidy and retains moisture. However, it is not essential; the mound can be built straight on top of the soil or even on concrete. Where the mound is to be built directly on soil, any grass should be mown or strimmed and the ground covered with damp cardboard. If the mound is to be built in a trench on a grassed area, the grass should be removed carefully as turves, which are set aside for use later.

As with a normal trench composting system, the mound is best started in the autumn so that it will be ready for the new growing season in the spring. The soil dug from the trench is kept for use as the top layer of the completed mound. If the mound is being made in a previously dug part of the garden, it will be necessary to obtain turves from elsewhere or to omit the turf layer.

The trench is dug, normally in a north-south direction, about 1.5m (5ft) wide and 30cm (12in) deep. It can be as long as the compostable material available permits. The mound will shrink, so it should be built higher than the desired final height of the bed.

Once the trench has been dug, a border of logs, boards or stones may be constructed around it, to frame the bed and keep it tidy. Alternatively, a more natural mound may be built without a frame.

Because of the inclusion of the wood, the mound will initially be low in nitrogen, so it is important to include nitrogen-rich materials such as manure, kitchen waste or grass to help fill the gaps between

Hügelkultur mound: woody material to be buried in the base of a small demonstration.

Small Hügelkultur mound finished with a compost layer and ready for planting.

Initial woody material for the Hügelkultur mound, covered with twigs and soil.

reached (remembering that the mound may shrink by a half during the first year).

The soil removed when digging the trench is then used as a final layer to cover the pile. If the mound is built correctly, the heat released by the decomposition will warm the soil, helping to extend the growing season.

The technique can of course be varied to suit different situations. A mound can be made by digging a trench, as above, about 30cm (1ft) deep, putting hardwoods in the bottom followed by soft woods, with the wooden portion being covered with twigs and small prunings. Manure, straw and the usual uncooked kitchen and garden waste are then added. Depending on the proposed use of the area, the soil and the turf removed when digging the hole are then added.

As the wood decomposes during the first year or two, the mound will shrink. If it is important to maintain the initial height, additional layers of greens and compost can be added.

If a site is unsuitable for a mound, the technique can still be used, with the ground being kept level or slightly sunken. A trench or ditch is dug so that the logs can be buried as deeply as possible, and the greens and other materials are added as if building a mound, but stopping at ground level.

logs and in subsequent layers. The material should be watered well.

If turves have been saved, they should be placed upside down (with the soil/roots up) over the woody material, forming a domed cover. The turves and each subsequent layer should be watered as they are added. The turves are in turn covered with a layer about 20–30cm (8–12in) thick of garden waste, leaves and the usual compostable materials. As with the woody layer, the larger items are deposited first. This layer is covered in turn with a 10–15cm (4–6in) layer of semi-mature compost or manure. These layers can be repeated until the desired height is

CHAPTER 6

MID- AND HIGHER-RANGE COMPOST BINS

There will come a time when a single entry-level bin will not be sufficient, and the keen composter will need to either purchase more similar entry-level bins or upgrade to larger bins that will be capable of composting a greater quantity or a wider range of materials. In many cases, there will be larger models in the same range or of the same construction as the entry-level bins. The less adventurous composter and those happy with what they are already using may simply buy additional items or upgrade to a larger bin of the same type. However, if a decision is taken to expand, it is worth looking at the different designs that are commercially available. At the basic level of the mid- and higher-range bins, there are wooden versions and home-made bins of a similar capability, while at the more expensive end are insulated bins designed for hot composting – the technique that involves regularly turning the organic material to produce weed- and pathogen-free compost more quickly (see Chapter 7)

Wooden Bins

Ideally, a wooden bin should be at least 1 x 1m in size and, if it is planned to be used for hot composting, at least a metre (3ft) high. The size is important because the larger the volume of the composting material the better the heat generation and retention. In some of the more extensive country-house gardens, the sides of the bins might be as high as 2.5m (8ft). The height of commercially available wooden bins varies according to each manufacturer and smaller bins can certainly be used effectively when cold composting. One of the reasons for having lower sides is that, if the bin contents are to be turned manually, the risk of back pain is reduced where the working area is at or below waist height. When deciding on the height of a bin, it is wise to consider all factors involved in manual handling: the weight of a loaded manure fork, the frequency of lifting the load, and any twisting involved in moving the compost from one bin to the next. Traditionally, 1000-litre capacity bins have been available, measuring a cubic metre, but there are now bins as large as 1200 litres with a height of 750–900mm, which may give a more comfortable working zone.

If the timber is pressure-treated (tanalised), it should last between 15 and 20 years. Sometimes, wood is sold as 'treated', but it has only been painted with preserving chemicals. This type of wood will deteriorate over time and may need to be retreated with preservative every other year to prolong its working life. There is a possibility with some older treatment products that chemicals may leach out of the wood into the compost and then pass into plants that are grown in the compost when it is added to the garden. However, with modern 'eco' preservatives there are fewer environmental implications than in the past and the risk to humans is not significant. If there are concerns, bins may be constructed from untreated wood, but these will have a shorter life.

When choosing a wooden bin, it may have slatted sides, giving better ventilation, or solid sides, which provide better insulation and heat retention. The boards on the side and back panels are often screwed in position while each board in the front panel slots individually into place, allowing easy access when loading, turning or harvesting the compost. Some modern bins have slot-and-drop panels on all sides, allowing easier access.

Sinking the bottom 15–30cm (6–12in) of each corner post into the ground will add to the stability of the bin. If it is likely that the bin will need to be moved, the posts can be stood on the ground. Corner posts designed for a slot-and-drop structure make it easier to extend the bin to make a two-, three- or four-bin system. A lid or compost duvet cover will help control the moisture level and retain the heat.

One of the advantages of a traditional-style compost bin is that the organic material can be seen in its layers, which makes it easier for the user to ensure the correct ratio of greens and browns. The ability to open the front means that the layers can be turned easily once a week (starting a few days after the bin is filled)

Double wooden bin with solid sides.

A wooden bin made of decking, with slatted sides. The slats in the front panel are removable.

Wooden bin, lidded and lined.

for the first month, or just left to compost slowly, depending on the technique adopted. The second and possibly the main advantage of this type of bin is that it can be home-made from a variety of woods, of different quality and longevity, depending on the materials and budget available. Those materials can range in quality from old pallets, which can be obtained free of charge, to repurposed treated wood such as decking, and in size from the pallets right up to railway sleepers for really large bins.

If the contents of a traditional-style garden compost bin are not going to be turned, it is possible to use the method of 15cm (6in) layers of garden waste alternated with a manure activator, or another activator. Each layer is levelled before adding the next. The garden waste should be chopped or shredded into small pieces and levelled with the back of a fork or a rake. On larger bins up to about 3 x 3 x 2.5m (10 x 10 x 8.5ft), the composter can climb in carefully and tread the material level with their feet. The bin is covered to keep it dry and retain heat until the compost is finished, which should be in about six months.

Plastic Bins

Traditional-Style Bins

There are plastic bins similar in design to the traditional wooden bin available for the home composter. The corner posts are held in position by relatively short 700mm galvanized ground spikes hammered into the ground; the user needs to be aware that these can move out of alignment with time.

It is possible to have a conventional-style bin made of the same recycled plastic from which park benches and other items of public-space equipment are manufactured. These are much heavier and sturdier than those plastic compost bins of a similar style that are made for the domestic market and come with a 25-year guarantee. They can be supplied with a lid and have the feel of a bin that is built to last.

The heavy-duty triple bin in the same range, supplied in a bank of three, is suitable for hot composting. It provides a cost-effective, zero-maintenance system for professional and communal gardeners who would like visitors to be as impressed by the quality of the composting facilities as they are by the end product.

Tekplas plastic bin: the tops of each upright can be lifted off to allow removal of the slats.

Heavy-duty Callis recycled plastic bin made to the same robust standard as a park bench and guaranteed for 25 years. The bin has a two-piece lid.

Moulded Plastic Bins

When moving on from entry-level bins, there are slightly more expensive moulded plastic bins available. These are similar to the entry-level models but may have additional features such as a hinged lid, sliding doors, adjustable ventilation and a ground plate. Bins of this type are not designed for batch composting and should be started with two buckets of fresh compost from another bin. If fresh compost is not available, soil may be used. The bin is emptied by using the hatch and a spade or fork to remove small amounts or, for larger volumes, by removing the barrel from the base plate, exposing the bin contents.

Sectional Bins

Sectional compost bins are quite popular and, while some of the lower-priced entry-level bins of this type do not appear to be very robust, there are some very substantial mid-range models. Decent sectional bins will survive on demonstration sites for several years, despite being assembled and moved a number of times, and being handled by the public.

Komp

In addition to the entry-level sectional Komp 250-litre bin, the Komp range also includes small bins up to 400 litres and medium-sized bins of between 450 and 900 litres. At the top end are the larger Komp sectional bins, which can hold up to 2500 litres of material. All are easy to load, with most having a two-part hinged lid, and easy to empty by lifting the pin and opening one of the bottom sections. The Thermo Komp bins are also available in a range of sizes right up to 2000 litres.

The bins can be obtained with four, six or eight sides, depending on size and model. A six-sided model is used on the Stokes Wood demonstration site, clearly showing some of the advantages of the mid-range sectional bins.

Four-sided sectional bin with hinged lid. The bottom panel is open, showing the easy access to the finished compost.

Examples of sectional bins: four-sided, six-sided and slatted.

Garantia

Garantia offers sectional bins that range from entry level to premium, with capacities up to 1000 litres, including the Eco-Master, Eco-King and Thermo-Star. They are operated in the same way as the cold-composting bins in the entry-level section. The bins should, if possible, be mounted directly on the soil in a sunny or semi-shaded, well-ventilated position. A base can be fitted if rodent access might be a problem.

An Alternative Design of Plastic Bin

Alternative designs of plastic bin include the Green Johanna, which consists of bands that are screwed one on top of another. This bin can be used for cold composting, but it will also hot-compost cooked food (*see* below).

Large sectional bin in use on an allotment. It is quite common to use stones to hold the bin lid shut.

Sectional bin with two of the bottom panels open, allowing easy emptying of the bin.

One section of the hinged lid on a six-sided sectional bin shown opened. The whole lid can be removed.

Premium Plastic Bins

Biolan, based in Finland, is a premium manufacturer that produces a range of quite expensive compost bins with a number of interesting features. The 900-litre Biolan garden composter is suitable for large private and public garden usage and is insulated for year-round composting. The bin can be fitted with a rodent-proof base and has an adjustable ventilation valve. It can be lifted off the compost for harvesting.

The smaller 450-litre Hotrock Garden Composter is suitable for kitchen and garden waste from a large family. It is a rodent proof hot-composting system and suitable for animal waste. It is designed to give the appearance of a large stone. It has air distribution tubes supplying air directly to the central core of the compost mass.

Biolan garden composter.

The 'Stone', one of the Biolan range of composters in a garden.

Mixing Bins

Gravity-Fed Bins

Gravity-fed bins – for example, the Earthmaker and the Exaco/Juwel Aeroplus 6000 – are not widely used or available, but the idea behind them is interesting. They are designed to mix the compost with minimum effort, so they are easy to use. The bins have different levels that separate the waste, with each level holding compost at different stages of decomposition. Fresh uncooked kitchen and garden waste is fed into the top level and after about four to six weeks will have dropped to the second and lower layers.

The fall aerates and mixes the waste and during the second stage it may heat up to 60–70°C, killing seeds and weeds. After about six to eight weeks, it is aerated and mixed again as it is moved down to the bottom compartment, where the composting process is completed.

Gravity-fed Earthmaker bin. The composting material is put into the top chamber and then pushed down to the lower chambers.

Tumbler Bins

Compost tumbler bins are available in three basic shapes: horizontal drums, vertical barrel-shaped drums and round drums, which are rolled on the ground or turned on a ground-mounted base. Small tumbler bins are available in the entry-level price range, but these tend to be less robust than the mid-range bins.

The bins that are rolled on the ground or in a base to rotate the contents can be heavy to turn, depending on their size. When selecting one of these bins, it is advisable to check that the body posture that will be

Vertical and rolling tumbler bins are heavier than the horizontal versions to turn when full.

A rolling tumbler bin. Larger bins such as this can be heavy to turn when full.

required while turning it is not too awkward for the user. The vertical barrel-shaped bins may be easy to turn when empty, but they can also be heavy and difficult to deal with when half full. Some vertical bins have the draining holes at the top when they are at rest, with water draining into the lid and then being tipped out when the bin is rotated.

One of the mid-range bins available is the metal horizontal Mantis, which is mounted off the ground on a frame, allowing the waste to be emptied directly into a wheelbarrow. The models with larger drums are often crank-operated to make turning easier. The drum may consist of a single or double chamber and will normally have internal baffles to help mix the materials. With the twin-chambered models, material can be maturing in one chamber while fresh material is added to the other. However, a separate maturation bin is recommended for maximum production and to make best use of the speed at which the material is broken down.

It is beneficial when composting in a tumbler bin to ensure the right mix of greens and browns. The process may also require the use of bulking agents when composting food waste. A mix of 40–50% carbon-rich browns should avoid the waste becoming wet and smelly, which is an issue that may occur with an excess of green, nitrogen-rich material. While batch composting is not essential, better results tend to be achieved if the organic material is added to fill the bin in one batch, turned a few times to mix and then left for three days to allow decomposition to start. It is then turned daily, if possible, for three weeks or until the compost is ready. However, the bins can be very forgiving and the system will work with materials being added in small quantities; it will just take longer to produce the finished compost.

Vertical tumblers: the two on the right come to rest upside down with the drainage holes facing upwards.

A tumbler bin together with a range of entry-level bins on an allotment.

A Mantis horizontal metal tumbler bin, which is turned by means of the handle and can be emptied directly into a wheelbarrow. Metal bins are more expensive than plastic but are more resistant to rodents and longer-lasting.

Woodchip, sawdust and proprietary mixes can all be used as a source of carbon and as a bulking agent. Another advantage of these bins is that they are sealed containers mounted off the ground, which reduces the risk of rat infestation.

Bins for Composting Cooked Food Waste

It is estimated that about one-third of all the food purchased in the UK is thrown away and that at least half of the discarded food was fit to be eaten at the time it was discarded. In the past, food waste presented problems for the composter as the waste tends to be dense and wet, and is prone to become very smelly. If it is composted in a conventional heap or plastic bin, it may also attract flies and rodents.

There are modern hot-composting bins on the market that are designed for the composting of cooked food waste from households and small businesses, in addition to garden and other waste. These can produce compost in around six to eight weeks. They are operated in the same way as the normal compost bin, with material being added as it becomes available. The difference is that material needs to be added two or three times a week in order to obtain the required temperature. Composters of this type include the Green Johanna, Hotbin, Biolan, Jora (Joraform), and the smaller Ridan models. They are usually insulated and may be used in conjunction with a maturation container to store the compost while it matures. This is a good way of increasing the through-put of the composting vessel.

The larger, more expensive food-composting systems for communal composting, such as the larger Ridan, Big Hanna, Jora 5100 and Rocket, produce compost on a 'continuous through-put system', where materials are added daily at one end of the composter and finished compost removed at the other end.

The systems designed for composting the food waste from a domestic setting or a small business can be located in the open on a hard, easily cleaned surface and do not require any services, such as electricity. Larger communal systems may require an electrical supply and will therefore need to be kept under cover.

In the case of food waste, which is high in nitrogen and water, there will be a need for a carbon source to provide the composting microorganisms with energy and add structure (or bulk) to maintain sufficient air spaces for aerobic composting. The usual range of materials can be used as bulking agents during cooked food composting, including wood chips, wood pellets, sawdust, wood shavings, dry deciduous leaves, shredded garden waste and animal bedding. On agricultural properties, other readily accessible materials such as hay, wheat straw and corn stalks may be used. The most suitable bulking agent will depend on the composting container and the nature of the food waste being processed. The quantity required will also vary. Many recommend 2 parts bulking agent to 1 part food waste.

Green Cone Food Digester

The Green Cone is not a composter and does not produce compost, but is specifically designed as a domestic food-digestion system for waste such as cooked vegetables, pasta, meat, bones and dairy products. A limited amount of pet faeces can be added, but it is not designed to take garden or non-kitchen food waste. The cone will take a 5-litre kitchen caddy of waste every two to three days during the winter and every one to two days during the spring and summer. However, this will depend on the type of food being added and on environmental conditions. The cone requires a sunny location so that it can provide a 'heat trap' of circulating air to encourage bacterial growth within the food waste. An accelerator powder, consisting of bacteria on a cereal base, will need to be added regularly during the winter months.

It is possible to use a Green Cone successfully for a number of years, but potential users should be aware that, as the waste is broken down to water, carbon dioxide and soluble nutrients, the digestion chamber must be buried in well-drained soil. In clay soil conditions, the hole in which the basket is buried can be enlarged and the basket surrounded by gravel and small stones to improve drainage and prevent the contents becoming waterlogged.

A limited amount of solid residue is produced by the cone, which is said to require removal at two- to five-yearly intervals, but this depends very much on its use. Some owners find that they never need to empty the basket, even after a decade of use.

It is important that the Green Cone is not overfilled, as the waste material should be kept within the

The Green Cone food digester is not a compost bin. The food is broken down underground and the liquid produced drains into the soil.

underground basket. Overfilling is probably the main cause of problems with the Green Cone. Generally, when a cone seems not to be working, it is because the operating instructions have been ignored and it has been filled to the brim with waste, including garden waste.

Green Johanna

The Green Johanna is a hot-composting bin that can be used with a wide range of food waste including bones, bread, dairy products, eggshells, fish, fruit, meat, vegetables, coffee filters and teabags, as well as garden waste. An insulating jacket can be purchased to help keep the contents active during the winter. During the summer the extra insulation provided by this jacket will also help maintain the 40–60°C temperatures required for hot composting. The Green Johanna can be used to compost the waste from a family of five to eight people. The bin or bins should be located in a sheltered, shady part of the garden, perhaps tucked away by a chicken run, so that the bedding from the chickens can be added directly. The disadvantage of such a location is that it may attract rats, but they usually fail to gain entry, even though they may attempt to dig underneath. Bins like these have also attracted the attention of badgers on the demonstration site, but

A Green Cone food digester dug into the ground (right) and the black inner cone and underground basket (left).

A Green Johanna and an Aerobin 400 compared for size. Both are suitable for composting kitchen and garden waste.

they have not been able to do more than simply chew the handles of the lid.

The Johanna is at its best processing 2 parts food waste to 1 part garden material. The garden and food waste should be added in layers, with each layer of food waste being covered with a layer of garden waste (if possible, chopped or shredded). Wood shavings from a chicken hutch may also be used. An aeration tool is provided to manually aerate the upper layers every time new material is added. As there is relatively little garden waste available during the winter, it may be advisable to set aside autumn leaves and prunings for use over this period. Sawdust, shredded paper or cardboard can be used as a source of carbon instead of browns from the garden.

Green Johanna with a layer of greens (grass) added before being mixed with a brown.

The Green Johanna composts garden and kitchen waste including cooked food. An insulated jacket maintains the hot-composting temperature.

Green Johanna with grass and paper mixed together.

Green Johanna with chicken feathers (a green).

Green Johanna.

Green Johanna almost full with a green layer including tomatoes.

Full Green Johanna topped with shredded paper (a brown).

Hotbin

The standard Hotbin is supplied in 100- and 200-litre sizes, and 450- and 700-litre versions have recently been added to the range. It is designed for the year-round composting of garden and kitchen waste, including cooked food. It will take fruit and vegetable peelings, leftover meals, plate scrapings, meat, fish, small bones, teabags, bread and cakes, in addition to garden waste. The Hotbin is made of insulating mate-rial (polypropylene) and if used correctly will operate at 40–60°C, reaching 70°C on occasions.

The compost bin is fitted with a thermometer so that the temperature at the top of the bin can be con-stantly monitored. An additional thermometer may be purchased, to allow the temperature of the compost lower down to be measured. A ventilation flap (valve) is also fitted to allow the temperature to be moderated.

Regular monitoring of the temperature provides an indication as to when fresh food needs to be added; this should certainly be done when the compost cools to less than 40°C, but the routine addition of about 10 litres of material weekly is recommended. As an example, the bin should be fed the contents of a 5-litre caddy twice a week plus two to three handfuls of shredded paper and one to two handfuls of wood chips as a bulking agent to help maintain airflow. This gives 1 part woodchip to 10 parts food waste.

It is relatively easy to keep the Hotbin operating during the winter, provided it is fed regularly. The Hotbin lid thermometer measures the temperature of the steam rising from the composting material and, unless the bin is over half full, it will record a temperature 10–20°C below that of the most active part of the com-posting material. A long-stemmed thermometer should be used at 2–4in (5–10cm) below the surface to obtain a more accurate measurement of the working temperature in the most active layer of waste.

A pair of Hotbins at Stokes Wood demonstration site. These are used to compost communal garden waste and food from the café.

Hotbin showing the large hatch and the thickness of the insulation.

Aerobin

Originally, the Aerobin 400 was not recommended for composting cooked food, but this advice has now changed. It can be supplied as a 200-, 400- or 600-litre bin and is suitable for hot composting. The bin has insulated walls to retain the heat generated during decomposition.

This hot composter will compost a large quantity of food waste, operating at a temperature that will kill potential pathogens, weeds and seeds. As a hot composter it can take meat and fish in moderation. It should be stood on a solid base, not directly on soil. The key feature is an aeration core inside the bin, which uses a patented 'lung' to circulate air. This promotes aerobic composting so there is no need for additional aeration or turning. The organic waste should be premixed before being added, to avoid concentrations of any individual material. Once this has been done, it can be dropped into the bin and left to decompose. When adding fresh garden waste that has not been premixed, such as waste from a reception bin, small amounts can be added at a time and mixed with the surface material in the bin using a hand fork or trowel. Take should be taken not to damage the lung.

The Aerobin 400, an insulated sectional bin with an aeration core which uses a patented 'lung' to circulate air and promote aerobic composting.

The Aerobin air circulation system does away with the need to turn the contents manually.

As with other bins, prior to the first loading of waste a layer of twigs or dried leaves, or a 10cm layer of compost from an active bin, should be spread over the base. This is followed by greens and browns, mixed before being added or added in layers. The thickness of the layers can vary between 4cm and 10cm (1.5in and 4in). Any paper or cardboard added to the bin should be scrunched up into balls. One suggestion, which can be used on other composting systems, is to insert 10–20cm (4–8in) strips of cardboard vertically into the material to create air pockets.

The bin works best if it is loaded to at least half capacity. The leachate produced is collected in the bottom of the bin and can be drained off for use as a liquid feed.

Biolan

In addition to bins for garden waste, Biolan also makes bins that are suitable for composting food waste. The 220-litre bin for year-round composting of kitchen and organic household waste will take the residue from 15 to 30 meals a day, along with garden and animal waste. It uses similar air-conditioning technology to the Biolan garden composters and can produce compost within about six weeks. The larger Biolan 550 food-waste composter, with a capacity of 80kg of waste per week, is suitable for use by schools, small businesses, restaurants, pubs and hotels.

Biolan 220 quick composter.

Joraform Composters

The Joraform (or Jora) range of composters will deal with all types of food waste, cooked and uncooked (including meat products). They range from the 125-litre, designed mainly for domestic use, to larger models for restaurants, schools, and other establishments.

The waste should be added to the unit frequently (every day or two) in small quantities. The composting drum on these machines is designed to rotate, mix and aerate the food waste with the sawdust or wood pellets that are added as a carbon source. The mixing also brings the fresh waste into contact with already decayed material, accelerating the composting process. One turn of the unit with each new quantity of waste is sufficient to aerate the contents.

The drum is insulated to retain the heat generated by the microbial activity. The high temperatures and even heat distribution mean that immature compost will be available in six to eight weeks.

Sawdust (in a ratio of one to three with waste), wood pellets (1:10 pellets to waste).or woodchip are normally added to the waste as a carbon source and bulking agent. Other bulking agents such as coir, dry leaves and dry, chopped straw can also be used.

The chamber of the Jora units is divided into two compartments, enabling the compost in the first compartment to mature while the second is being filled. The first can then be emptied out, ideally into a maturation bin, for further improvement before use. This allows continuous composting. A 125-litre Jora is excellent for turning uneaten sandwiches from a café into compost.

One of the insulated chambers of the Jora food composter.

Jora twin-chamber food composter. The smallest model in the range is used for food waste from a large household or small café.

Two larger, newer models in the Jora range, now marketed in the UK as Joraform food composters.

Ridan food composter in use.

Ridan Composters

The Ridan in-vessel, constant through-put thermal food waste composters range from the small Ridan, which can compost 80 litres per week, to the larger version that has a through-put of 400 litres per week. They are suitable for use in a variety of settings, from small schools up to commercial kitchens, cafés, restaurants, colleges and community schemes.

Food waste is cut into small pieces and drained to remove excess fluids, then loaded at one end, and an equal amount of woodchip, sawdust or shavings is added. The handle is rotated at least six times. Waste travels through the tube-like body of the Ridan, passing through the stages of hot composting before automatically emerging from the outlet at the other end into a bucket. The machines take equal quantities of greens, such as raw and cooked food, and browns, such as dry woodchip, which acts as a source of carbon and as a bulking agent.

Ridan also offers two Compostbox products for families of four and groups of up to 10. These insulated compost bins are designed for home composting of food waste. These are similar in shape to some other domestic food composters but have stainless-steel cases and foam insulation to retain heat throughout the year. Material is added from the lidded top and harvested from a hatch at the bottom.

Maturation

In nearly all cases, once the food waste has been composted it is best to transfer it to another container for a further two to three months before use, to create a really good growing medium. Special maturation bins are available for purchase, but separate pallet bins or redundant plastic models can also be used for this purpose.

CHAPTER 7

COMPOSTING FOR THE ENTHUSIAST AND THE PROFESSIONAL

Composting Larger Quantities

Most composters start their composting career with an entry-level cool composting bin (*see* Chapter 5). Once they have become hooked on the process and realised the value of the end product, many will continue cold composting but add more entry-level bins, while others will progress to mid- or higher-range bins. Some will set up systems for hot composting food and mixed garden and household waste, in single commercially available bins. A few may find that they need to compost larger quantities of waste, and that they want to kill weeds and pathogens and exercise more control over the process.

Traditionally, large country houses and estates would have had a row of hot-composting bins adjacent to a walled garden, staffed by a team of full-time gardeners. Less grand houses with a large garden would probably have had a similar system with smaller bins, although 2.5m (8ft) bins were still turned by hand. Similar set-ups using three or four smaller bins were then adopted by allotment gardeners and form the basis for the advice given here.

The country estates are now staffed by fewer gardeners, assisted in some cases by volunteers. While the working bins may not be as pristine as they once were on all estates, there will be many that are managed using modern equipment and techniques. The gardening staff and volunteers are usually more than happy to discuss their procedure and provide a good source of composting knowledge. The busiest and most productive composting areas may have restricted access, but a keen composter can usually obtain permission to have a look. At the National Trust property of Clumber Park in Nottinghamshire, for example, there is a bank of five bins turned by tractor and the composting area is included in some of the garden tours. As with other sites where the material is turned by tractor, the material to be composted is not cut into short lengths as the turning requires no physical effort.

On some estates, the composting systems have been modernised, mechanised and enlarged and form part of a wider 'green' agenda. One such estate is Blickling Hall in Norfolk, where the National Trust has added new bins to the composting yard and invested in a biochopper, which mechanically chips and mixes the organic waste in order to increase through-put.

Today, those with large gardens, allotmenteers, managers of community composting schemes and

Compost bins on a National Trust estate. Bays of this size can be turned using a tractor or by a team of volunteers, or left unturned.

The first two of a bank of five bins at the National Trust property of Clumber Park, in Nottinghamshire, using brought-in compost and woodchip.

Maturing compost.

Bin being filled.

Compost ready for use.

Part of the composting area at the National Trust estate of Blickling Hall, showing the old bays.

Part of an active composting area.

Mixed organic material.

Equipment used to cut and mix organic waste ready for composting. Cutting and mixing speeds up the composting process.

The shafts are a key part of a composting shredder and should be able to grind and mix the organic waste.

Bins used to deal with compostable waste at Leicestershire County Hall, setting an example to other organisations considering how to deal with their own waste in-house.

enthusiastic composters will all be operating a similar system, some using tractors to turn the waste and some with smaller bins where the material will be turned by hand. Leicestershire Council is one local authority in the UK that is setting a good example to householders, having built a bin system that is turned by tractor to compost organic waste produced at County Hall.

Hot Composting

Traditional hot-composting techniques are good for dealing with the waste from a larger garden, allotment or community composting site, where there is a significant quantity of organic material and a quick through-put is required. The less professional composter can also replicate this type of system by

A three-bay garden-sized bin.

constructing a traditional layered bin to provide favourable composting conditions. Achieving a good end product through this method is very rewarding, as is managing the temperature by turning and mixing the contents.

Using hot composting, it is possible to produce immature compost in as short a period as 21 days, or in six to eight weeks, depending on the method chosen. Hot composting typically involves a bank of three or four bins – although single bins can be used – and has the advantage that thermophilic bacteria will generate sufficient heat to kill weeds, seeds and pathogens. It also denatures or degrades some pesticides and herbicide residues and discourages rodents.

Bins on an individual allotment. They could be used either for hot composting, turning from one bin to the next, or as individual cold bins.

Many triple bins seen on allotments are used as individual bins rather than for turning as part of a hot-composting system.

Productive bins on an allotment, with one of the plot-holders.

A three-chamber wooden set-up, complete with a marrow growing in one of the bins.

Part of the community composting site at Stokes Wood, showing pallet bins used for hot composting.

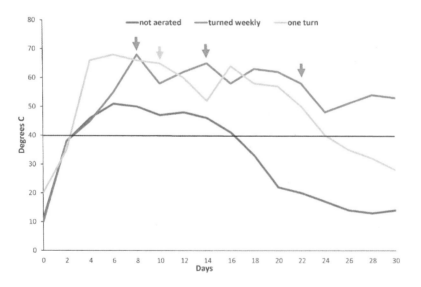

Temperature patterns for bins under different management regimes, showing the benefits of aeration. The temperature will be dependent on a number of factors, but turning tends to increase it and prolong it at the higher level. Under some conditions, a large 'no-turn' bin can reach 70°C by relying on passive aeration, but a lower temperature is more typical for this type of container.

Wooden bins can be purchased and put together to create a productive bank of three or four bins, but they may also be constructed from discarded pallets, allowing the waste to be turned as part of the aeration process. With bins made from pallets, the waste can be shredded in advance or cut up as it is added to the bin. Using long-handled shears will reduce the need to bend. With larger bins it will be less labour-intensive to chop and mix the waste by mechanical means prior to adding it to the bin.

Microbiological Stages

A working knowledge of the microbiological stages of hot composting, and the practical implications of those stages, is not necessary when cold

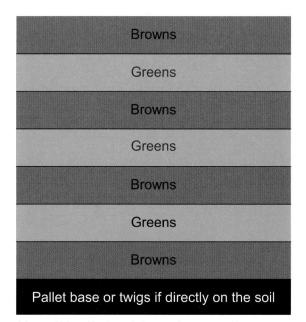

Browns
Greens
Browns
Greens
Browns
Greens
Browns
Pallet base or twigs if directly on the soil

A layered bin, with alternate layers of greens and browns from household and garden waste The layers provide an easy means of estimating the C:N ratio when filling the bin. The materials can be mixed by turning after two or three days.

Topped with soil or woodchip
Activator e.g. seaweed
6" Vegetable waste
Activator e.g. soil
6" Garden waste
Activator e.g. nettles
6" Garden waste
Activator e.g. manure
6" Garden waste
Activator e.g. coffee
6" Garden waste
Activator e.g comfrey
6" Garden waste
Three-sided bin standing directly on soil

composting. However, it is essential to have an understanding of the science when hot composting using traditional bins.

Psychrophilic Stage

During the winter, the compost heap may become frozen and even on warmer days the temperature may not rise above 13°C. Psychrophilic micro-organisms function at low temperatures, from -10° to 18–20°C (14–68°F), but below about 13°C most of the microorganisms in the heap will be semi-dormant and decomposition of the material will be limited. The best advice is to insulate the bin and leave it undisturbed.

At 13–21°C, the psychrophiles become more active but they produce only a small amount of heat compared with other bacteria. Indeed, they can be active throughout the winter without significantly raising the temperature. Good insulation will help retain the heat generated and, as the weather becomes warmer, the heat they produce can be sufficient to increase the temperature of the heap or bin. As the temperature rises over 25°C, the psychrophiles are denatured and the mesophiles become important to the process.

The temperature will follow a basic pattern as the material passes through the composting process. The actual temperature and length of each stage will be dependent on a number of factors: the management system, materials, bin size, and so on. In the immediate aftermath of turning there will be a dip in temperature, but ultimately it will result in a higher bin temperature for a longer time.

Mesophilic or Initial Stage

The mesophilic phase is the first phase of real composting. The initial mesophilic stage normally lasts for two to four days, with the temperature ranging between 20 and 40°C. When hot composting, recording the temperature provides evidence that the bin is

Bin layering system suitable for a large garden or allotment, where the vegetable waste is alternated with an activator, for example, a sprinkling of farm manure, fish, blood or seaweed.

active, and that the temperature is rising through the mesophilic stage to the thermophilic. Keeping the bin covered helps retain the heat. Details of some of the bacteria, actinomycetes and fungi involved are given in the tables below.

It is best to batch compost, filling the bin in layers on one day or at least within a week. A little longer can be allowed if necessary, but the sooner the bin is filled the sooner the turning and aeration can commence.

Thermophilic or 'Active' Stage

During the mesophilic and thermophilic stages of the composting process, most actinomycetes and fungi are confined to the outer 5–15cm (2–6in) of the heap or bin. Some moulds also grow in this zone of the composting galaxy. Unless the compost is aerated by turning frequently, hyphae can give the area a greyish-white appearance. With aeration the cooler material in the outer areas is turned into the centre of the heap, ensuring that all the material reaches the higher temperatures in the core. This will prevent the formation of sufficient hyphae to produce the colour change and the 'burnt' appearance that may be seen in no-turn compost systems.

Thermophilic organisms start to dominate the heap at temperatures of about 40°C. The higher tempera-tures in this phase allow for the breakdown of proteins, fats and complex carbohydrates such as cellulose and hemicellulose. The length of time the phase lasts – from a few days to several weeks – will depend on what is being composted, the ratio of greens to browns and the management system.

The thermophilic organisms continue generating heat by decomposing the remaining organic matter. As this food source is used, the activity of the microbes declines and the temperature in the compost will start to fall. Aeration and mixing the organic material at this stage results in the exposure of the organisms to fresh food, increasing the microbial activity and extending the period for which the material is held at sanitising temperatures.

Table 7.1 Bacteria that may be found in compost

Name	Habitat
Alcaligenes faecalis	Intestinal tract of vertebrates, decaying materials, dairy products, water and soil; human respiratory and gastrointestinal tracts. May cause opportunistic infections
Arthrobacter	Soil, aerial surface of plants and wastewater sediments
Bacillus species	Species of this saprophytic genus are found in soil, water and a wide range of other environments. Some are associated with infections of wounds and disease. B. stearothermophilus is thermophile (heat resistant)
Brevibacillus brevis	Soil, air, water and decaying matter
Clostridium thermocelium	Found in plants and animals. In the digestive system of cattle and horses, for example, it breaks down the cellulose of grass
Enterococcus	Opportunistic pathogen
Escherichia coli (and other Enterobacteriaceae)	Human and animal guts. Some are pathogenic, causing diarrhoea or other illness. Pathogenic E. coli can be transmitted through contaminated water, food and by contact
Flavobacterium sp.	Found in soil and water
Pseudomonas sp.	Different species are widespread in water, plant seeds and a wide range of locations. P. Aeruginosa can be a human pathogen and often causes ear infections in dogs. P. syringae is a plant pathogen
Serratia sp.	Widespread in the environment, S. marcescens can be pathogenic
Streptococcus	Some species are part of normal gut flora, some are pathogenic
Thermus sp.	Found in soil, faeces, meat, sewage and thermal springs
Vibrio sp.	Some are aquatic, some pathogenic

Table 7.2 Examples of actinomycetes and compost fungi

Name	Description and habitat
Frankia	Nitrogen-fixing bacteria. About 15% of the world's naturally fixed nitrogen is found in species of *Frankia* and their host plants
Streptomyces	Filamentous bacteria with an earthy smell, producing vegetative hyphae and spores. Found in soil and decaying vegetation. Some species are pathogenic to plants
Other actinomycetes (at least 14 species have been identified) incl. *micromonospora*	Some are anaerobic. Decomposers of tough plant tissues such as the cellulose and lignin in bark, paper and stems
Aspergillus fumigatus	Fungal mould. Soil and decaying organic matter – compost, bird droppings, tobacco, stored foods. Can grow at temperatures up to 50°C and survive at 70°C (conditions found in hot composting)
Basidiomycetes sp.	Mushrooms, toadstools, rusts and smuts. Important in the degradation of lignin
Humicola grisea, H. insolens, H. lanuginosa	Thermophilic fungal mould. Soil and plant material. Common in compost
Malbranchea pulchella	Thermophilic. Soil, decaying vegetation, dung
Myriococcum thermophilium	Thermophilic. Compost, soil, manure, agricultural residues, stored grains, industrial coal mines
Paecilomyces variotii	Thermophilic. Composts, soils and food products
Papulaspora thermophilia	Thermophilic between 41 and 122°C. Hot springs, hydrothermal vents, peat bogs and compost
Penicillium sp. (incl. *P. dupontii*)	Grows at 15–27°C. Compost, soil, food, the air and dust of indoor environments
Scytalidium thermophilum	Thermophilic fungus. Used in the production of mushroom compost
Termomyces sp.	Thermophilic fungus 52–53°C. A dominant fungus of compost heaps at high temperatures
Tricoderma sp.	27–30°C. Soils and other diverse habitats. Increase the rate of plant growth and the production of roots

Members of both groups contain filamentous species and play a role in breaking down the tough plant residues such as cellulose and animal residues.

Turning the contents also provides an opportunity to check that the conditions continue to be appropriate (*see* Chapter 3) and to water the bin if the moisture content has fallen too low. However, turning should not be done too frequently, as this may reduce the level of nitrogen and organic material.

Eventually, the food source will be so depleted that the temperature will continue to fall despite turning, allowing the return of the mesophilic organisms as the dominant group of bacteria. This third and final step in the composting process is known as the curing, maturation or conversion phase. Unmatured compost can be used as a mulch, but it is usually preferable to allow the compost to mature further and wait until the next season if possible.

Curing or Maturation Stage

For the curing or maturation stage, the technique can be as simple as leaving the compost in the bin where it completed the second mesophilic stage, moving it to a spare pallet bin or entry-level 'Dalek' bin, or making it into a covered pile. It is also possible to purchase a dedicated maturation bin, such as the Ridan Pro 400 maturation box.

At this stage of the composting process, the easily degradable organic materials will have been utilised. The remaining material (including chitin, lignin, humic materials, some remaining cellulose, starches and proteins) is not soluble in water and cannot be absorbed into the bacterial cell due to its chemical complexity and size. The actinomycetes and fungi now come into the picture, as they can degrade these compounds using extracellular enzymes that allow them to be absorbed. As they act on the materials, they also liberate carbon, nitrogen and ammonia, making nutrients available for higher plants. They are especially important in the formation of humus – organic matter that has reached the final state of decomposition – and are responsible for the earthy smell associated with compost. First appearing five to seven days after the start of the composting process, actinomycetes develop into large clusters. As they assume their role during the final stages of decomposition, they work on organic materials that are tough to break down, such as avocado seeds and glossy leaves, and may also produce antibiotics that inhibit bacterial growth.

To avoid breaking up the hyphae of actinobacteria (and fungi), tumbler composters should not be turned during the curing phase. Similarly, compost in conventional heaps, piles or bins should not be mixed or aerated.

Fungi also play a significant role during the final stages of composting. They are primitive plants that can be either single-celled or many-celled and filamentous. They are present in smaller numbers in the compost than actinomycetes or bacteria, but are larger in body mass. Their main contribution to a compost pile is to break down cellulose and lignin. They prefer cooler temperatures of 22–24°C and easily digested food sources. During the curing and maturation stage of composting, the cooler temperatures also encourage the entry of worms, insects, mites and other macroorganisms.

The time of the curing process can vary. A longer maturation is desirable as it allows the levels of humus in the compost to increase, as well as reducing the likelihood of pathogens and phytotoxins being present. It may also prevent the development of organic acids, which will limit the use of the end product as seed compost. A period of between six months and two years is recommended, depending on the materials being composted. If the content is woody, a longer maturation period will be necessary, to allow more time for the lignin to be broken down.

Hot Composting Using Traditional Bins

When hot composting using traditional bins, it will be necessary to have easy access to the bin in order to turn the material. For example, a bin of one cubic metre will require at least 1.5 x 1.5m of space around it. The area should be well-drained, level and, if possible, located so that it does not get dried out by too much sun or waterlogged by heavy rain.

Wooden bins for hot composting can be made using old pallets, planks, decking, railway sleepers or scaffold boards. Brick or cement blocks can be used to make permanent bins. If the bins are to be emptied or turned by mechanical means a concrete base may be advisable but if not a soil base is preferable.

A bank of bins is the usual set-up for traditional hot composting. A single bin can be used, with the waste being turned within the bin, although it is better to remove it on to a plastic sheet as if this was a second bin. It is also possible to hot compost with a single bin without turning if it is large enough.

It is usually recommended that bins for hot composting should be at least 1 x 1 x 1m, to retain the heat produced by the microbial activity. Larger bins up to a height of 2 to 3m (6–9ft) can be used, but turning by hand in such bins becomes difficult, making the use of a tractor necessary. Alternatively, the bin can be layered in such a way as to maintain internal air circulation, and not turned. If the bin is too large there is a danger that the weight of the material will compress the bottom layers, which will then become anaerobic. With larger bins there is also a risk that the temperatures may rise too high, killing some of the composting microbes in the organic material. Sometimes, the materials may even spontaneously ignite.

The bins can have a slot-and-drop boarded front, which retains the compost and allows access in the initial phase when the contents are being turned regularly and later, when the bin is being emptied. Bins may also be built without a front.

Pre-Composting Storage

Traditional hot-composting systems use batch composting, with the organic material being added to fill a bin as soon as it is collected or within a few days of collection. Where this is not possible it can be saved until there is enough to fill the compost bin in one or two sessions. This may make it necessary to have some pre-composting storage space.

Saving the materials to fill a bin is best achieved by having separate storage bins and dry space for each type of material. Some materials such as shredded paper, cardboard and woodchip are easily stored in sealed dustbins. As long as they are kept dry, the materials will not decompose during the storage period. Straw can be left in bales or bags and covered. It can be chopped immediately before use to speed the composting process.

Autumn leaves for use as a brown are best stored dry in polythene or dustbins to be added to the hot-composting bin during the late autumn and winter. Shredded woody prunings, and brassica and similar stalks can be stored in an empty plastic or wooden compost bin. Some recommend using a compost pit and keeping the materials slightly damp by allowing moisture to penetrate. This will make them easier to compost. The stalks will need chopping or shredding before being added to the bin.

Freshly cut grass clippings are high in nitrogen and if stored directly in a bin may decompose quickly, forming a dark, wet, smelly anaerobic mat. This can be avoided by allowing the clippings to dry out completely before adding them to a storage bin. When storing vegetable, herbaceous or bedding plants and flowers and other green garden waste, two bins can be used. One should be allocated for coarse materials such as stalks, finished annuals and pot plants, and the other for green vegetable matter. Materials such as annual weeds, green manures and water plants removed when clearing ponds are best exposed to the sun to dry for a few days to reduce their moisture content before storage. Once it has dried, this green waste can then be stored in a bin until required. Small quantities of fruit and vegetable kitchen waste can be stored in a refrigerator or freezer. If they are stored outside in the garden, fruit and vegetables will start to decompose quickly, although the rate of decomposition will vary. A little compost placed on top of the waste will reduce odours during storage.

Traditional Hot-Composting Methods

Hot composting involves more work than cold composting, but that makes it more rewarding, as the efforts of the composter contribute to the quality of the finished product and speed of production. The method begins with covering the base of the bin with a 15–20cm (6–8in) layer of twigs, sticks or stalks to assist in creating airflow through the contents. Although these will be distributed throughout the pile once it is

turned, they may survive intact until the finished material is sieved. Woodchip or cardboard can be used as an alternative base material – emptying a bin with these items incorporated is easier than shovelling sticks. Filling the bin using alternate layers of brown and green materials – about 7cm (3in) for greens and 2.5cm (1in) for brown – provides a visual means of monitoring the quantities added to the bin.

When home composting it is relatively simple to collect greens and browns separately, but with mixed garden waste it is often easier to use layers of the waste alternated with layers of activators such as manure, seaweed, comfrey, soil or compost. When looking to achieve hot composting, it is not necessary to start the greens and browns in separate layers, however, as they will be mixed regularly when the material is turned and aerated. There are alternative systems in which the greens and browns are premixed. Some National Trust estates grind and mince larger quantities of green and brown waste by machine, using a ratio of approximately 40% of greens and 60% of browns. Home composters can also premix the materials before adding to the bin.

Most hot-composting systems involve adding the organic material in a batch, to fill or at least half-fill the bin on a single occasion. Normally, a bank of bins is used so that the material can be aerated by turning from one bin to the next. In the basic hot-composting system, the bin is filled with green and brown materials that have been cut or shredded into small pieces of 2.5–5cm (1–2in), exposing a larger surface to microbial decomposition. Water should be added as the pile is

A base layer of twigs and stalks will allow the air to enter at the base and circulate up through the bin contents.

Cardboard and brown paper make a good base layer where the material is to be turned regularly in the first week.

A layer of comfrey – a green activator – about to be cut to size.

The first green layer being positioned to be cut to size.

Layer of fresh weeds including nettles.

Hedge clippings, mainly leaves, deposited in a bin as a green layer.

Layer of matured cow manure (a green activator).

Shredded paper provides a source of browns.

Autumn leaves used as a brown layer are best shredded.

Brown layer of torn cardboard.

An almost full layered bin covered with cardboard overnight to make the cardboard wet and easier to tear.

Used paper towels added as a brown layer.

Soil can be used as a top layer or as a layer in the bin to introduce additional microbes.

built, usually after each layer and if the material is dry when it is turned. For the material to break down quickly, a moisture content of 50% is required.

There are variations on this technique, where layers of manure, mature compost or soil may be added as a source of more microorganisms, with or without additional greens such as nettles or comfrey as an activator. In the past, lime was added to the compost bin to reduce acidity, but unfortunately it also reduces the nitrogen content and is now used less often. However, when composting significant amounts of highly acidic material, such as pine needles, adding a small amount of lime can reduce the acidity and aid decomposition. If soil requires the addition of lime, it is better to add it to the finished compost immediately before its application rather than adding it directly to the soil.

Achieving, Managing and Monitoring Temperatures

The objective of hot composting is to manage the temperature of the material in order to prolong the thermophilic stage (*see* Chapter 3). One visual warning that the bin is too hot is provided by the growth of a white 'mould' that is actually made up of anaerobic thermophilic actinomycetes (a bacteria). If this appears, it may be necessary to cool the bin. This white bloom will usually disappear when the temperature falls.

When hot composting at home the composter should aim to maintain the temperature for 10 to 15 days. Larger and deeper heaps result in higher temperatures and better heat distribution throughout the pile, exposing more material to the required temperature. Using non-turn methods may result in the core material reaching thermophilic temperature but not the outer layers, although they will compost. Turning the material so that the outer areas of the bin form the new hot central core is the key to exposing all of the material to thermophilic temperatures. A single turning may be sufficient to hold the temperature at 60 or 70°C for the requisite number of days.

Turning the heap every two or three days from the fifth day to the fourteenth is labour-intensive but it will achieve higher compost temperatures than only turning every 10 or more days over a longer period. As a compromise, the contents may be turned weekly for three weeks. Turning fortnightly or monthly is less likely to maintain temperatures of over 65°C but does usually help to keep the temperature above 40°C for long enough.

Another way to manage temperatures is to monitor and measure the heat in the bin or heap, and base the frequency of turning on the results. If the temperature is recorded regularly, the compost can be turned whenever it falls below 50°C or rises above 72°C. Measuring the temperature of the compost may also help to determine when it has reached a temperature that is high enough to sanitise the contents, and whether that temperature has been maintained.

During the active thermophilic stage of decomposition, the temperature will fall a few degrees immediately after turning but it will rise again, reaching its original temperature within two or three hours. When using this system of monitoring to control the composting process, it is helpful to take additional readings three hours after turning. The turning may then be continued until there is no marked change in temperature following aeration.

The temperature record should include the date the bin was loaded, even if it was not fully filled on the first day. Measurements are best taken at three or more locations in the bin. In community composting the temperature should be recorded daily, if possible, to provide evidence of having achieved and held a suitable temperature. Temperature recording is most helpful during the first mesophilic and the thermophilic stages. Once the temperature falls to the second mesophilic stage, recording can be less frequent.

Two days after filling the bin the temperature will have reached 40°C, moving from the mesophilic to the thermophilic stage.

By the fourth day the temperature will be well into the thermophilic range, at 60°C.

When the temperature reaches 40°C, pathogens and seeds will be killed, but many composters prefer to operate at 60–70°C to be on the safe side. Ideally the temperature should not be allowed to rise above 76°C, as this will kill beneficial microorganisms. If the maximum temperature exceeds 72°C, it can be managed by turning/aerating to reduce it temporarily. If a pile does overheat, exceeding 72–76°C, many of the bacteria will be destroyed and the composting process may come more or less to a stop.

It has been found that during the thermophilic stage in some bins 87% of the organisms present were *bacillus* species, which are spore-forming. Most *bacillus* species are unable to grow above 70°C, but one species, *Bacillus stearothermophilus*, predominates at temperatures of over 65°C. Bacterial spores are formed as a survival mechanism and will go on to germinate when the compost cools to a suitable temperature. Other thermophiles that play a role in hot composting include the fungus *Rhizomucor pusillus*, which is active as the temperature rises but is inactivated at peak temperatures.

If the compost has been allowed to overheat to such an extent as to inhibit bacterial activity – reaching a temperature of over 76°C – turning will be less effective in cooling it. Watering the material is sometimes suggested as a means of reducing the temperature but this should be attempted with care, as there is a risk of waterlogging.

A fall in temperature during what should be the thermophilic stage may occur if parts of the material are becoming anaerobic. This may be accompanied by a fall in pH. It can often be rectified by increased aeration and the addition of more browns.

Eventually, there will be insufficient nutrients available to maintain the higher temperatures and the heap will return to the cooler levels of the mesophilic stage, even when turned. Some heaps show a relatively rapid fall to ambient temperature while in others it is more gradual.

Active Hot Composting

Hot composting involves more work than cold composting, but it is a method that will produce compost in a much shorter time (25–90 days). It is rewarding, too, as the composter is in a position to influence both the speed of production and the quality of the finished product. The key lies in getting the right mix of greens and browns. Alternating layers of the two is a simple way of getting the desired ratio but it does not help to overthink the process. While many use approximately equal amounts of each in 5–10cm (2–4in) layers, others use layers of about 7cm (3in) greens to 2.5cm (1in) browns to allow for the different density of the two and there are many other layering combinations.

Some composters find that mixing the two together in advance is more effective than layering. With the right machinery to grind and mince the green and brown waste, this can be most effective, using a ratio of 40% of greens and 60% of browns.

If there is a lack of high-nitrogen material, a small amount of commercial fertiliser containing nitrogen can be added at a rate of 125ml of fertilizer for each 25cm layer of material. Adding a layer of soil, which will contain decomposing organisms, will also help get the pile off to a good start.

It is relatively easy to monitor and control the stages of composting where waste is added in batches and turned regularly, as temperature changes can be made to apply to most of the heap. The outside layers become the new central core, while the original hot core is moved to the sides and top. If the material is not turned, the higher temperatures will occur only in the central core. Where a tumbler bin is being used, the mixing and aeration will occur with each turning. When hot composting in a single bin, adding material two or three times a week – for example, using a Green

Johanna, Hotbin or Ridan Compostbox – only the upper layers of the composting materials are turned, as it is in this layer that thermophilic temperatures are reached. (The lower layers will be at mesophilic temperature as the composting is completed.)

The bin or heap should be covered, to restrict evaporation, retain heat and prevent the material becoming waterlogged during wet weather.

There are mixed views on the number of times a heap should be turned. A single turning may be sufficient to eliminate the pathogens and parasites, but for this to be effective all the outside material must be completely turned to the inside and it will need to be left for several months. Most hot composters will turn material at least twice, but many will opt for more turns – maybe three, four or even five – to be on the safe side. Another approach is to go for a rapid composting system, turning every two days for the first two weeks. This should quickly produce immature compost. Alternatively, turning can be carried out whenever the temperature falls below 50°C, until there is no marked change in temperature following the aeration.

The recommended turning technique involves taking the material from around the edges of the first bin to make the central core of the new bin. Material from the hotter central core of the first bin is then used to form the sides and top layer of the new bin. This ensures that the cooler edges of the bin during the first period are heated in the hotter central core during the second period. This method of aeration is continued until the temperature remains unchanged after turning.

The result of turning a bin is that the top and outside layers become the new central core.

The Berkeley Method of Hot Composting

The Berkeley method, developed by the University of California, is used to make immature compost in only 18 days, with 1-metre-square bins filled with organic materials to a height of 1.5m (5ft). The first bin is filled with alternate layers of green and browns with a layer of comfrey, nettles or old compost added to the middle of the heap as it is built. The contents are gently watered until water drips out of the bottom of the pile. On the fifth day the contents are turned into a second bin and again every second day. The peak core temperature of 55–65°C will occur between days 7 and 9 with the process usually ending by the seventeenth day. The compost can be moved to a maturation bin on day 18. A variation of this technique involves daily turning, which is said to result in compost being produced in just two weeks.

The moisture level of the contents should be adjusted during aeration, with water being added as necessary, taking care to avoid waterlogging, as this will cool the contents and may result in the formation of undesirable anaerobic patches. Combining pH readings with temperature checking is an optional extra for the enthusiastic composter.

Monitoring the temperature and turning the materials is continued for about a month or until the temperature has fallen to below 30°C (depending on ambient temperatures). By this time, most of the material will have turned into dark, crumbly compost, and there will be no increase in temperature following turning.

No-Turn Hot Composting

It is possible to hot compost in a traditional bin using alternative layers of combined garden waste and manure activator without turning, and still reach temperatures of over 70°C. No-turn methods are slower to act than those in which the material is aerated regularly but will still produce compost in about six months. Larger bins are preferable, ranging in size from 1.25 x 1.25m (4.5 x 4.5ft) to 3 x 3m (10 x 10ft), depending on the size of the garden. The bins can be up to 2m high and left open-fronted for ease of access. The sides can be slatted, with 25mm (1in) ventilation spaces between the planks, or solid, to provide insulation.

A 15cm (6in) layer of garden material is laid directly on the soil and raked level. A 25–50mm (1–2in) layer of mature manure activator or about 100g of fish manure is then added, followed by alternative layers of waste and manure until the bin is full.

Waste from the garden and the kitchen can be mixed together in 15cm (6in) layers consisting of items such as the tops of beans and peas, torn-up leaves of cabbages and sprouts, crushed stalks of brassica, weeds, grass, fruit and vegetable peelings. Eggshells, woollen and cotton scraps, soaked and torn-up newspaper, dried leaves and a little sawdust can also be added as part of this layer.

This type of layer is alternated with a manure 'activator' layer, using any suitable waste, from farmyard animals, poultry, pigeons, rabbits and other vegetarian pets. Fish, blood or seaweed were also commonly used as activators when this technique was widely used. The top of each layer is levelled so that the contents heat up evenly. A layer of soil, about 25mm (1in) thick, is added to the top, and the bin or heap is covered to help retain the heat and to prevent the contents becoming waterlogged.

For the no-turn technique to work, the bin must be well constructed, with adequate air spaces, and moisture levels must be maintained. The effort required for no-turn is certainly low, and a fairly extensive set-up could include a larger layered no-turn bin, which should produce good compost in about a year. The

The composting material in a larger bin during turning and aerating.

When harvested, compost from a no-turn bin may be lumpy compared with product that has been turned and broken up regularly.

contents may be lumpier than from a bin in which the contents have been turned and broken up several times. If some weeds survive, they can be dealt with by hoeing.

Curing or Maturation of the Compost

When the compost no longer heats up when turned it is ready to be 'cured' or matured. During this stage, the compost becomes dark, crumbly and takes on

Turning and aerating a larger bin using garden forks.

A bank of pallet bins containing maturing compost covered for the winter months. The moisture level should be checked monthly as well as the sides of the bin for evidence of rodent entry.

The finished product from home and garden composting may contain eggshells if they are not crushed when first added.

Section through the compost in an over-wintered bin.

Finished compost may contain small pieces of wood and occasionally small stones from plant rootballs.

A batch of compost from a pallet bin to be used a mulch still containing some wood, the remains of the original base layer.

Compost maturity can be tested by sealing a sample in a bag and checking how it smells after three days.

a pleasant earthy smell. This process usually takes at least eight to 12 weeks. Some composters prefer to leave it to over-winter, in order to have it ready for the start of the new growing season. Maturation can take place in the final bin if using a bank of bins, or it can be moved to an old 'Dalek' bin, a specially designed maturation bin or even a covered heap.

It is recommended that the compost be checked during the maturation process. If it shows signs of drying out, it should be sprayed with water. It is usually not necessary to turn the maturing compost, although some suggest that it may benefit from being aerated every couple of months. If the material is too wet, however, turning will be necessary.

There will be some shrinkage during the maturation process and the pH should settle at or near to neutral (pH 7). Some items – for example, corn cobs, egg-shells, teabags or woody material – may not break down fully. These materials can be removed by passing the compost through a sieve or screen, with the objects that are extracted being added to a new compost pile.

A simple test as to whether the composting process is finished is to put a scoop or handful of the compost in a plastic bag and seal it for three days at room temperature. If when opened the contents have a pleasant, earthy smell, composting is complete. For more information on testing, *see* Chapter 12.

CHAPTER 8

POTENTIAL PROBLEMS

Good compost should have a pleasant and earthy smell, a dark appearance and a fine, crumbly texture. Unfortunately, things can go wrong in the time between the ingredients being added to the bin or heap and the expected harvesting of the final product. There may be issues with the limited breakdown of some materials, the temperature or chemical make-up of the contents, and interference by vermin and other animals. Fortunately, there is generally a technique that can be employed to rectify any problem.

Issues with pH Levels

Acidic Compost

Sometimes, an excess of greens can upset the pH balance of the compost, turning the contents acidic and smelly, and slowing the decomposition. The addition of large amounts of acidic ingredients such as citrus fruit or the decomposition of excess food can also contribute to an excessively acidic compost bin.

The optimum pH for compost microorganisms is in the range of 5.5 to 8 (see Chapter 3), although in vermiculture the worms prefer a neutral soil in a narrower range (pH 6–7). Compost tends to become slightly acidic during the early stages of decomposition due to the formation of organic acids. These conditions favour the growth of fungi and the breakdown of lignin and cellulose in the plants. The organic acids become neutralised as the decomposition proceeds and by the final maturation the pH will range from 6 to 8. If the compost is too acidic, adding calcium carbonate materials such as crushed eggshells or wood ash may help to neutralise it. Agricultural lime (for example, dolomite and crushed limestone) used to be recommended to neutralise acidity, but this is no longer advised as it results in the release of nitrogen gas. After adjusting the pH, it may be necessary to add additional green material to kick-start the composting process again.

Acidity can also be reduced by removing rotting food that has not been absorbed, adding additional bedding or improving airflow by turning and mixing. If the heap does not respond in the right way, it may be necessary to dig it out completely on to a polythene sheet and turn in additional coarse browns to absorb moisture and create air spaces. After mixing thoroughly, the compost can be returned to the bin. The smell should disappear in a few days and the compost will continue with its aerobic decomposition.

Rainwater should not be a problem with a lidded bin or tumbler, but it is worth checking for leaks if the material is very wet without any other obvious cause.

Alkaline Compost

Alkaline compost is not often a problem as most compost becomes slightly acidic at an early stage. However, if the material does become alkaline, remixing the contents should adjust the pH. Adding grass clippings or green vegetable leaves may be helpful.as they can increase acidity.

Insects, Bugs and Other Creatures

Ants

Ant infestation is a common problem in compost heaps and bins, especially in hot summers, when ants and their nests seem to get everywhere. Often it is said that it occurs when the compost is too dry but in the right conditions, ants will set up home in even quite moist wormeries. They may also be attracted by exposed and uncovered kitchen scraps in the top layer of a bin. Small numbers of ants present in the bin are beneficial in that they bring fungi and other organisms into the compost and can add phosphorus and potassium. They also help to produce a finer compost. However, it is best to discourage them from nesting. This can be done by keeping the bin moist and maintaining the temperature above 60°C by turning regularly (which will also destroy any existing nests) or adding greens. Soaking the bin or nest seems to work for some composters.

Bees and Wasps

Compost bins provide a nice sheltered space for bees and wasps, which may be found nesting under the lid. Where possible, they should be left undisturbed, and another bin or heap started if space permits. The colony will usually die after a few weeks, after the queen and males have emerged, or at least by the autumn, when the bin can be returned to use.

If it is wasps that are nesting and the bin is required for use, the municipal authorities or a removal service

An ants' nest in a 'Dalek' compost bin, showing the eggs and the fine compost produced.

may be contacted. Occasionally, a swarm of honey bees will get into a bin. In this case, the advice is always to leave them undisturbed and abandon the bin for the time being, or invite a local beekeeper to take them away. It is not recommended to call an exterminator, as they will probably dispose of the bees by killing them.

Flies

Chopping plant materials and kitchen scraps into small pieces and storing them in a closed caddy excludes flies, while an open container provides easy access for egg laying and a means of introducing fly eggs into the bin. Food waste should be buried in the compost or covered with a layer of browns. The top layer in the bin should always consist of browns and it is advisable to use a layer of shredded paper on a lidded bin and soil or woodchip on an open bin. If a lidded bin is used, the lid should always be replaced to maintain a fly-proof cover. If flies are a problem, ventilation holes in a plastic bin can be best covered with a mesh screen to prevent access. A heap can be covered with a tarpaulin or plastic sheet.

Both uncooked and cooked food waste can attract flies, wasps and rats.

Whitefly on brassicas should not be a problem in the compost bin. Although the eggs on fresh material may hatch, the flies will die.

Whitefly

Infestation with whitefly is not unusual in plants to be composted. The flies are not a problem as they live on sap and once the plant is dead it will not provide food for them. In summer, when fresh green and kitchen waste is added to the compost heap, flies may lay eggs in it. When they hatch, they may form a fly-cloud each time the bin is opened. If this is a problem, it can be resolved by simply covering the compost with a layer of soil, spent compost or other browns.

Maggots

A few maggots can be beneficial as they break down food waste into a form that is easier for worms to digest. However, a large infestation is not very pleasant, and they will compete with the composting worms for nutrients. Black soldier maggots, for example, can eat twice their body weight daily. Likely to be present in subtropical and tropical areas of the USA, Europe and Australia, these scavengers thrive on decomposing organic matter, so are common in compost heaps and can be used for breaking down household waste.

Maggots may also be a sign of too many greens, resulting in too high a moisture content. To discourage them, the waste should be turned regularly and additional browns – for example, cardboard, dried leaves or straw – mixed in. They may also be controlled by a rise in the compost temperature and the presence of predators such as beetles.

Grass Snakes and Slow Worms

A compost heap or bin provides shelter for grass snakes and can also give them a perfect place to lay their eggs and rear their young in safety. Snakes are attracted to compost bins where the contents generate a small amount of heat, such as a bin containing mainly dry browns and some moisture. Slow worms (a legless lizard) are also often found in compost bins and heaps in the UK. Both grass snakes and slow worms are harmless, and the usual advice is to leave the bin undisturbed until any eggs have hatched, and the young have moved on.

Snakes and slow worms may be less interested in a bin or heap that has the correct balance of greens and browns, and where the contents have the right

Spot the slow worm. Slow worms and snakes may be occasional visitors. The advice is to leave them undisturbed.

Evidence of a badger digging for food in an open-fronted bin.

Badger damage to a wire-netting bin for making leaf mould.

moisture level and are aerated regularly. It is advisable to learn to distinguish the harmless snakes from the venomous.

Animals

Badgers

Badgers can do considerable damage to a garden and lawn, gaining access through gaps in the hedge or by digging under fences. They are creatures of habit and, once a garden is on their route, they will visit it regularly. They are protected by law in the UK, where it is illegal to trap, harm or kill a badger, or to interfere with its sett.

Badgers will be attracted to the contents of a compost heap or bin as a source of nourishment, particularly if it contains cooked meat or dairy products. Uncooked vegetable and fruit matter will also interest them, along with composting worms. Burying or covering any edible kitchen waste in the compost with dry leaves or soil is not very effective at masking the smell and badgers are still likely to detect it.

Once they find their way into a garden there is usually nothing to prevent badgers gaining access to a compost heap or pile and helping themselves, so the first approach should be to try to stop them from entering at all. LED lights triggered by infrared sensors can be effective, at least until the badgers get used to them. There are a number of other methods that are reputed to deter these creatures (some of which are more practical to consider than others!):

- a 'smelly' washing line at badger height, hung with cloths impregnated with various oils, including citronella, clove, eucalyptus, menthol, juniper berry or wintergreen;

- Scotch bonnet peppers, chopped or crushed and scattered on the ground;
- human (male) urine, diluted and sprayed around the plot every four weeks; and
- lion manure.

If none of these works, it may be necessary to adopt a policy of learning to live with the badgers and trying to defend the composting area or bin itself. Compost bins are easier to seal against invading badgers than open heaps. If it is not possible to replace the heap with a bin, a badger-proof fence will need to be constructed around the area. Surrounding a bin with paving slabs or large stones can help to stop a badger digging into it from below. A 'Dalek'-style plastic bin can be protected by thick wire mesh being fitted across the base. Bins designed to take cooked food will usually include an integral base. If the bin is supplied with a sliding hatch, this can be secured shut with a single screw. The common clip-in hatches can be protected by weldmesh screwed in place. If the lid is easily opened, it will need securing.

Tumblers mounted on a frame off the ground should be relatively safe from attack, although the smaller, lighter models are best pegged in position as they may be knocked over if only partly filled. Metal bins are more resistant to badgers than plastic ones, and a wooden lid offers better protection than a tarpaulin or plastic sheet cover. Mounting a wooden bin on slabs or fitting wire mesh across the base can prevent entry. Depending on the quality of the wood, the sides may also need protecting with wire mesh. This should be sealed around all the edges, or it can be mounted on a frame to fit the sides of the bin and screwed in place, allowing it to be removed when easy access to the bin is required. If a bin is to be protected by netting, this can be buried in the ground and stapled to a wooden base board.

Rats

Rats are commensal rodents whose numbers are influenced by human activity, buildings and created landscape. Some activities – composting using open heaps, keeping chickens and feeding garden birds – may attract rats, while others such as keeping cats or terriers may discourage them. Although many gardeners and composters will rarely, if ever, see a rat, a fear

Composters encounter different problems in different countries: this tumbler successfully resisted the efforts of a bear to gain entry.

of attracting them is one of the most common reasons given for not home composting.

Tunnels in the soil around the site or holes chewed in the side of a bin are often the first sign of the presence of brown rats. Burrows are normally about 3–4cm (1.25–1.5in) in diameter and may be seen under the bin. Shredded paper or other dry material brought into the heap or bin is probably evidence of rats nesting in the compost.

The contents of a dry compost bin make a good restaurant for rats, which have a preferred diet of cereals, nuts and fruits, meat and fish. Rats are also attracted to compost bins and heaps as dry places to shelter and nest. The compost bin will be particularly attractive during the winter, providing warmth and a good supply of food, with kitchen scraps being regularly added to the top while the material in the lower part of the bin is relatively undisturbed. Rats need to gnaw hard surfaces to keep their teeth under control as they grow throughout their lifetime, so many wooden and some plastic bins will offer little resistance if a rat smells the decomposing food inside.

Bin Location

As the brown rat prefers to move along runs close to walls, fences and hedges, bins should be positioned in the open. Leaving space around the bin also makes it easier to check for any burrowing. Black rats tend to like trees and shrubs, so it is best to place the bins away from these. If trees do overhang the bin, the lower branches should be cut so that they do not provide a means of reaching the bin.

Material Being Composted

Rat infestation of a compost bin may be linked to the composting of bread, cooked foods, dairy products, fish, meat, fatty and processed foods. While eggshells are undoubtedly appealing to rats – some composters

Rat damage to a Hotbin hatch – the first and only incidence in 10 years. It might have occurred because the hatch had not been refitted properly.

Bins situated close to a fence are likely to be directly on or adjacent to a rat run and are more likely to be found by them.

A rat burrow into pallet bin. This is quite common during the winter if the bin is not being turned. Turning the contents should discourage infestation although an occasional visit cannot be avoided.

Signs of a rat burrowing under a Green Johanna. The bin is fitted with a base, making it much more difficult for the rat to gain entry.

A layer of pebbles being used to discourage rats burrowing into composting bins not fitted with a base plate.

even recommend washing them to reduce the smell before adding to the bin – other more basic kitchen waste such as fruit and vegetable peelings will also provide an appetising meal once the rats have gained access. It seems that rats are quite keen on potato peelings and the smell of decomposing fruit certainly seems to attract them to many schools' compost bins and food digesters. If fruit waste has been removed from the bin and rats are still regular visitors, it may be necessary to stop adding vegetable waste from the kitchen until the compost has been emptied, and the contents replaced with a higher proportion of garden waste, and turned more regularly. However, simply adding more garden waste may not solve the problem – rats can also be attracted to bins containing plant trimmings and weeds.

Human Intervention

There is some anecdotal evidence that the number of times the heap is disturbed can influence whether it becomes infested by rats. It is certainly true that rats do not like frequent or continued disturbance. Putting the bin near the house or by a garden path that is used regularly and knocking, kicking or hitting the bin with a stick every time it is passed certainly makes it a less desirable residence for rats.

Vermin and Plastic Bins

Regular aeration of plastic bins using a commercially available compost aerator or garden fork is helpful as it disturbs the deeper layers of compost. Regular turning of compost being made in New Zealand or pallet bins has the added advantage of maintaining the temperature of the contents, at least during the initial stages of composting. In a multi-bin system that includes a maturation bin, the compost in this final bin should also be turned, particularly if it is being left for some months.

Vermin and Wooden Bins

A solid-sided wooden bin is obviously more secure than one with slatted sides. Slat-sided bins can be made more rat-proof by lining the inside with galvanised 13 x 13mm wire mesh or making a separate frame of mesh that can be attached to the outside and

Physical barriers to rats

Sometimes it will be necessary to use physical barriers to prevent rats gaining access to a compost bin. They often find a way in through the soil on which the bin is stood. There are several ways in which this risk can be reduced:

- Laying a solid concrete base not only provides a solution to this problem but also makes it easier to shovel up the compost from the bottom of the bin. Ideally, the base should be sloped slightly so that the leachate runs into a gulley leading to a buried bucket. This can then be used as a compost activator or liquid feed (see Chapters 9 and 13).
- Paving slabs can provide a less permanent solid base. They must be laid touching each other so that the rats cannot get in between them.
- Removing a layer of soil and laying a 10- to 15-cm (4- to 6-in) gravel base into which the bin can be placed can be quite effective, especially if used with a weldmesh base fitted round the bin.
- A weldmesh or other metal mesh base can be fitted across the bottom of the bin. Chicken wire is not recommended, as rats may chew through it. The size of the mesh is important as rats can get through a gap as small as 15mm (half an inch). The advantage of wire mesh over concrete stands is that it allows worms access and makes drainage easy, although the leachate also drains away.
- When buying a plastic bin, it may be possible to add a base as an extra. These normally contain small drainage holes, which also allow worms to gain access.
- A metal tumbler bin mounted up off the ground offers good protection from rats.
- Traditionally, a bin would have been covered with a tarpaulin or carpet. However, to be more certain of keeping rats out, a secure, tight-fitting lid is necessary. With a square bin, where the lid is the type that pushes or drops into place, rather than fitting over the rim of the bin, there must be a tight fit. If there is any gap between the sides and the lid, rats may succeed in enlarging it in order to get in. As an additional precaution, against both rats and strong winds, the lid may be held in place with a bungee cord.

removed when emptying the bin. There is less risk of rats chewing their way into a solid-sided bin, but these may also be protected further by lining with mesh. If the bin consists of separate boards that can be lifted out one by one to give access, the separate removable frame will be a useful addition.

If the bin is not standing on solid concrete, the mesh should cover the base to exclude rats but allow easy access by worms. The lid should also be lined with wire.

Leptospirosis (Weil's Disease)

Care must be taken when working in areas contaminated by rats as they can harbour the bacteria that causes leptospirosis, as well as other potential pathogens. In humans, leptospirosis (also known as Weil's disease) usually results in mild flu-like symptoms, such as headache, chills and muscle pain. However, it can sometimes be more severe, causing life-threatening issues, including organ failure and internal bleeding.

Leptospira organisms are spread in rats' urine and can survive in water for several months. The risk of catching Weil's disease from contact with soil or compost recently contaminated by rats' urine is small, with fewer than 40 cases reported in England and Wales every year. Nonetheless, it is a good idea to wear gloves when handling garden compost, especially if there are cuts or grazes on the hands.

Temperatures below 4°C and above 37°C will kill *leptospira* bacteria, which have an optimum temperature of about 25°C. This means that they may survive cold composting but will be killed by hot composting, at 40–60°C. However, if they are introduced by rats later in the composting process, when the compost has cooled during maturation, it may survive.

In general, contaminated compost does not present a problem for growing food. Once the compost is applied to and mixed with the soil, the level of bacteria will be so low that vegetables grown in it will be safe to cook and eat as normal. However, if a cold-composting bin or heap is known to have been infested, it is probably advisable as a safety measure to use the compost in the flower garden or as a mulch round an established tree.

Temperature Levels

One of the most common concerns relates to the failure of the compost to heat up, with no obvious cause being identified. In many cases, it can be the result of the user adopting cool-composting techniques without realising that a different procedure is required for hot composting. Most of the compost bins that are commercially available are designed primarily for cool composting, so they are relatively small. Although they are supplied in a range of sizes, the most popular have a capacity of only 220 litres, or even less. The minimum size for a hot-composting bin or heap is about 1 cubic metre, to provide enough mass to retain the heat generated by the composting microbes. In addition, the shape of many of the most popular bins makes them unsuitable for hot composting, as it is difficult to fully aerate the contents. In cool composting, the organic material is added to the bin in relatively small amounts as it becomes available, which allows the active upper layers to be aerated as new material is added.

If the bin size and the ratio of greens to browns are right for hot composting, but the contents have still failed to reach the required temperatures, it may be because the material was not sufficiently moist when added to the bin or has dried out during hot weather. The situation can be rectified by adding water while turning. A sponge test should then be performed after allowing the water to be absorbed for a few hours.

If the compost has reached and held a working temperature and then started to cool again, it should be turned. If it does not respond to turning it may have completed the active stages of composting and can be put aside to mature.

If the compost has not managed to reach working temperature, it can be helped by the addition of nitrogen-rich greens such as comfrey or kitchen scraps. This will increase microbial activity and produce the necessary heat.

A temperature drop may occur during cold weather, so insulating the pile or bin may be necessary in winter. Suitable insulation for the side of a bin could include bubble wrap, hay, loose straw or straw bales, or cardboard. A heap may be insulated by arranging straw bales around it or covering with a black plastic compost duvet, sheet or tarpaulin.

Moisture Levels

Too Dry

If the compost bin is too dry (with a moisture content below 15%), it will stop decomposing as the bacteria and fungi responsible for the composting process will not be able to work effectively (see Chapter 4). Efficient activity is achieved when the moisture is maintained between 40% and 60%. Compost bin contents that are too dry may also provide a tempting nesting site for rats, mice, slow worms and grass snakes.

Too Wet

An excess of moisture is one of the most common problems encountered by the new composter, but it is easily rectified. Compost that does not heat up and has an unpleasant rotting odour is probably too wet or too densely packed because of too much fresh green material, such as grass clippings or vegetable peelings, being added to the bin.

Ingress of rainwater is an obvious cause of the composting material becoming too wet if it has been left uncovered during rainy periods. When the compost has been exposed to excessive rainfall the water passing through the heap will increase leachate, which will result in the loss of nitrogen from the compost. This

The result of too many greens is that the contents start to become wet and smelly. This is a sign that it is turning anaerobic. Mixing in browns will solve the problem.

can be replaced by the addition of manure, compost activators or a nitrogenous fertiliser if greens are not available.

Compaction in the compost results in poor airflow within the material and the filling of air in the spaces between the organic material with water, leading to anaerobic respiration rather than aerobic. A smell of ammonia from a wet compost heap may indicate too high a proportion of nitrogen-rich greens and poor air circulation giving rise to anaerobic conditions. When animal manure was commonly used in the making of compost heaps this problem was often associated with the use of urine-rich raw manure. The answer is to absorb the excess moisture and restore the correct C:N ratio.

The problem of excess moisture or wet compost can usually be rectified by turning or by mixing in more browns, such as cardboard, shredded or scrunched-up paper, sawdust, straw or shredded dried leaves, to restore the green:brown balance. Woodchip added as a bulking agent can also help create air spaces. If this does not work, the material can be removed from the bin and mixed more thoroughly on the ground. The problem can also occur where bulking agent has not been used to absorb the water produced by food added to the bin, particularly cooked food. Breaking up any lumps of food and mixing the material may be sufficient to solve the problem but if this does not work, additional browns should be added. Woodchip not only introduces carbon but also helps create air spaces in the organic material.

In the case of a tumbler bin, lumps may be a problem when the tumbler has not been turned often enough to break up the composting material, resulting in a lack of aeration. Turning the tumbler a minimum of two of three times a week during the initial stages will prevent this and will also aid the evaporation of excess moisture from the contents. If the pile becomes wet and anaerobic conditions develop, the organic acids may not break down and the compost will be too acidic. Mixing in additional browns and turning the compost will normally reduce acidity. If this fails, sprinkling handfuls of ground lime (calcium carbonate) or wood ash into the mix may adjust the pH; however, it may also cause nitrogen to be lost to the atmosphere, so is best avoided if possible.

Plastics and Packaging

Plastics in Compost

Plastic is widely used in many gardens and pieces may find their way into the material being composted. Strands from ground-cover fabric are a particular nuisance once they enter the soil. They are best removed manually, along with any other plastics, when making the heap, when turning and at the sifting stage, to prevent this.

'Compostable' Packaging

If 'compostable' bags and packaging do not break down properly, it will probably be because not all such packaging is home-compostable, and not all the items that are labelled as 'home-compostable' will cold compost. There are an increasing number of logos indicating whether and where packaging can be recycled and there is a degree of confusion between what is 'compostable' and what can be home-composted. If packaging carries the seedling logo and is described as 'compostable', it means that it is compostable in an industrial composting plant but cannot be composted at home. Only packaging that carries the words 'home-compostable' can be composted using a domestic composting system. It should be noted that the success rate for successfully composting different 'home-compostable' items is, to say the least, variable.

Pieces of plastic – from ground-cover fabric, plastic sheet, flowerpots, and other gardening items – are sometimes found in the material being composted.

The radish test: seeds are sown in samples of compost with a control sample to see whether the seeds germinate and grow to maturity.

Herbicides in Compost

If plants sown or grown in ground mulched or treated with compost show poor seed germination, poor growth and yields, death of young plants or underdeveloped or misshapen fruit, this can be caused by herbicides containing aminopyralid or clopyralid. When applied to hay fields or pasture consumed by horses and livestock, these pass through the animal's gut and remain active in the manure. Each batch of manure and compost should be subjected to the radish test: fill two containers, sow some radish seeds in it and see how many of them germinate. If three-quarters or more are successful, then the compost is ready for use. (Radish seeds are used because they generally germinate relatively quickly.)

Mould Growth

Although actinomycetes produce light grey hyphae and are often mistaken for fungi, they are actually bacteria. They are key to the composting process, belonging to the group of decomposers that help break down woody materials.

Actinomycetes are light grey in colour and give compost an earthy smell. They play an important role in composting.

The fungal mould *Aspergillus fumigatus* is commonly present growing on decomposing and decaying material, including in compost bins. It produces numerous spores, which become airborne when there is any physical disturbance of the material, for example during aeration or harvesting. The main risk to the composter is that they may inhale the spores, and that this may cause one of a group of diseases known as 'aspergillosis'. Not only does the fungal mould produce numerous spores, it is also able to survive thermophilic temperatures, which means that it presents an occupational hazard to those working in industrial composting facilities.

When turning compost that is dry, smells mouldy or has visible fungal spores, the risk can be reduced by standing downwind, moistening the material and adding a layer of shredded paper, which should then be soaked to prevent spores becoming airborne.

Acute aspergillosis following contact with decayed plant matter is rare, but those whose health is already compromised – asthmatics or people with a history of previous diseases such as tuberculosis – should wear a face mask of FFP2/FFP3 or N95 standard when working with composted material.

Odours

Aerobic composting, unlike the anaerobic process, should not create an unpleasant smell. Objectionable odours can come from certain raw materials or can be a result of the process itself not being properly managed. There are three primary sources of odours when composting:

- odorous raw materials;
- ammonia lost from high-nitrogen materials; and
- anaerobic conditions within the composting bin, heap or windrow.

Anaerobic conditions can be minimised by the usual proper management: using a good mix of raw materials, monitoring the moisture content to avoid an overly wet mix, managing leachate and rainfall run-off and turning to aerate the materials regularly. A high pH encourages the conversion of nitrogen compounds to ammonia, which further adds to alkalinity. Bad odours can be controlled by providing extra carbon in the mix and maintaining the pH below 8.5.

Moisture can be added by mixing in more greens (nitrogen-rich waste) and watering the heap or bin, preferably with rainwater from a watering can fitted with a rose. A little washing-up liquid may be added as a wetting agent. If possible, the material should be mixed to ensure the water penetrates all areas of the heap. If a two-bin system is being used, or there is a spare bin available, the materials can be turned into the second bin and each layer watered. The compost ingredients should feel about as wet as a damp sponge when squeezed. In a dry summer, a plastic bin is likely to need watering weekly to maintain the moisture level. A conventional cubic-metre bin will retain water more effectively but will still need some watering during hot, dry spells.

Some suggest using an oscillating sprinkler on top of a large compost heap for about an hour a day in very hot or dry weather, but this is discouraged as it leads to wastage of water as some will fall on the surrounding ground. Also, the use of sprinklers is prohibited on many allotments. The least-favoured option is to run a garden hose; if this is deemed absolutely necessary, the hose must be fitted with a spray.

After the contents have been soaked, it is advisable to check the material in the centre of the bin to ensure that the water has fully penetrated. Adding greens while turning and watering should reactivate the composting microbes and bring the bin back to life.

Invasive non-native plants

Landowners and gardeners in the UK have a responsibility to prevent the spread of certain invasive non-native plants into the wild and to stop them causing a nuisance. They must also prevent harmful weeds spreading on to a neighbour's property by controlling them in the most appropriate way. The authorities warn against composting many non-native plants because they can be very persistent and may survive the composting process. The end product may also infest areas where it is used. Unknown weeds should be identified before composting. Advice is available on the website of the UK Environment Agency (gov.uk).

Weeds and Seeds

Perennial Weeds

Some perennial weeds may be a danger to animals, or cause problems for agricultural production if left to spread unchecked. Others may just be a nuisance, as they will survive composting (*see* below).

Japanese knotweed is a particularly aggressive and invasive plant with an underground rhizome that may spread up to 7m along the ground and 3m deep. The shoots can even force their way through tarmac, causing structural damage to roads and houses. It must not be composted.

In the UK, other invasive perennial weeds include common ragwort, spear thistle, creeping or field thistle, broad-leaved dock and curled dock. While it is not an offence to have these weeds growing on land, the landowner must prevent these invasive non-native plants from spreading into the wild and causing a nuisance. They must also prevent harmful weeds spreading on to a neighbour's property by controlling them in the most appropriate way. Allowing contaminated soil or plant material from any waste to spread into the wild is an offence in the UK under the Wildlife and Countryside Act 1981, carrying with it a fine of up to £5,000 or a prison sentence of up to two years.

It is important to note that the fact that a plant can be composted does not mean that composting is the most appropriate way of dealing with it, as there is a risk of seeds surviving the process and allowing the invasive plant to spread. In the UK, the Environment Agency website should be consulted for advice.

Perennial weeds and seeds will normally be killed by hot composting where the temperature has been held at 40–60°C but they will survive cold composting. If using a cold-composting system, the weeds can be pre-treated by drowning, dehydration or light exclusion. If the compost is being used as a mulch, any weeds that have survived cold composting can be allowed to germinate and then hoed.

Drowning

Drowning is one of the quickest ways of dealing with perennial weeds and it has the added advantage of producing a liquid compost activator that can be poured into the compost bin or used as a liquid plant food.

The perennial weeds are put into a lidded bucket, old bokashi bin or water butt, depending on the quantity involved, and weighed down with a brick or stone. The weeds are covered with water, the lid put in place to exclude light, and the 'soup' left for between four weeks and a year or more. The time required will depend on the type of plant material. In the case of couch grass, for example, a year or longer might be required to kill all the roots. When all the plant material has broken down, the contents of the container can be added to the compost bin, or the liquid can be poured off carefully and sieved, then used as a liquid feed while the sludge is added to the compost. For more information on drowning plants and making liquid plant feed, *see* Chapter 13.

Mixed perennial weeds can be dealt with by soaking in a lidded dustbin until they turn into a sludge.

Drying

The drying method requires hot sunny weather to work most effectively. The weeds or their roots are spread on a dry flat surface such as a concrete paving

A weed-drying rack can be used to dehydrate perennial weeds before adding them to the bin.

Covering the weed-drying rack with a builders' bag will keep the plants dry and exclude light.

slab in full sun or a stack of recycled bread trays. Ideally, the roots should be smashed and flattened with a hammer to assist the drying process. They can then be left to dry for two or three weeks in hot sunny weather. Any plants that still have a large root ball containing earth may need to be left to dry for the whole season. After this, the roots will be sufficiently baked to be easily separated and safely added to the compost bin.

Light Exclusion

In this effective but slow method of killing or composting perennial weeds, they are put in a separate plastic compost bin and kept in the dark for two whole years to rot down. Alternatively, if space is limited, they can be stored in strong black plastic bags, away from light and air, for one to three years to degrade. Extra protection can be provided by covering the bags with a strong polythene sheet. The finished compost should be checked to ensure that no roots have survived.

There is a quicker method using plastic bags, but it is only suitable for use during the summer when lawns are mowed regularly. It involves mixing the weeds with fresh grass mowings in a plastic sack or bag such as an old compost bag. The bag containing the weed/grass mixture is tied up and left in a sunny spot until the weeds are no longer recognisable. Care is required when emptying the bags as the contents may be slimy.

Where perennial weeds are growing in turf or grass that must be cleared, as may be the case when taking on a new or neglected plot, a turf stack can be used. The turves should be lifted and neatly stacked, green sides together. The stack is then covered by a black plastic sheet and left for up to two years, by which time the grass and weeds will have rotted down to form a quality topsoil. This method can be used successfully to deal with couch grass.

Plants Growing in the Compost Bin

Cold composting will not kill seeds or perennial plants, but removing seed heads and separating perennial weeds and roots requires considerable time and effort. As a result, many composters do not separate them and simply add the whole lot to their cold bins. Weeds may even survive hot composting if the heap does not

Plants growing through vents in a sectional bin.

Weeds in compost growing out through the air gaps in a slatted bin.

reach and hold a temperature that is high enough to kill the seeds. If the compost is to be used as a mulch, it may be just as well to save time and effort trying to extract the weeds and seeds and simply invest in a hoe to deal with any weeds that grow in the composted area. In fact, compost bins or heaps are often used to grow plants such as marrows.

Issues with Worms

For more information on problems that might be encountered when using a wormery, *see* Chapter 10.

White Potworms

Potworms in a wormery are not a problem unless they swamp it, which may happen under certain conditions.

The easiest way to reduce the numbers is to add a slice or two of bread soaked in milk. This will attract the potworms and can be removed when covered in them. The conditions in the wormery can then be adjusted to favour the composting worms by doing the following:

- absorbing the moisture in the bin by adding dry compost, soil, paper, or other absorbent bedding;
- removing excess food in the trays;
- reducing the volume of greens provided; and
- adding lime or crushed eggshells.

Worms Dying

People often give up using a wormery because all their worms die. There may be several reasons for this:

- **Overfeeding**: this is a common problem with wormeries. If the food is not being eaten quickly enough it will smell and, in bad cases, form a soggy mess. If this happens, feeding should be stopped, to allow the worst of the mess to be removed and a mixture of damp cardboard and paper to be added. This will absorb the moisture and allow air to get in and circulate.
- **Adverse weather conditions**: in the summer, a wormery kept in the sun can easily reach temperatures that will 'bake' the worms. It should be in a shady area or shaded with a trellis or plants. Conversely, in the winter, the whole wormery should be insulated or moved to a shed or outbuilding. If it has a reservoir with a tap this can be left open to avoid the wormery becoming waterlogged.
- **Poor aeration**: the wormery will normally smell before a lack of aeration causes all the worms to die. If the situation is caught in time, cardboard and shredded paper mixed into the bedding will create air spaces.

Worms on the Lid of a Bin or Wormery

Concern is often caused when large numbers of worms appear at the top of the compost, on the inside of the lid and top of the bin or wormery, particularly when cold composting. Worms will gain access to any compost bin that does not have a base, that is to say, is open to the ground. Eventually, they will inhabit bins with a base and even tumbler bins where the drum is up off the ground. This is because worm eggs and casts are transferred on organic material from the garden being added to the bin. Once they have gained access, they play an active role in the composting of the organic material.

The worms cannot survive temperatures over approximately 35°C, so, when a hot-composting system heats up, they will move from the hot areas to any cooler zones. This means that they will be found at the base or in the bin lid, and they may even retreat into the garden soil if the whole of the heap exceeds the temperature at which they are happy. They will reappear during the cooler maturation, curing or ageing stage.

There are occasions when worms move up to the top of the bin in large numbers. This often occurs in the spring, when warmer temperatures result in those worms that have lived in the bin during the winter months breeding and producing a population surge. Worms may also be seen balling up together. They do this to protect themselves from various stressors: an unfavourable environment due to a rise in temperature

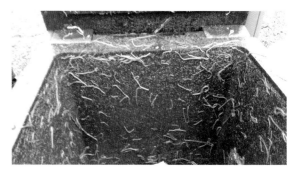

Worm 'escape' from the top thermophilic area of a Hotbin at a working temperature of 40–60°C. The lower levels will be cooler.

or changes in moisture levels, or any other alteration in conditions. Worms found at the top of the bin may also be escaping from overcrowding. In such cases, given a little time the population will usually balance itself out without any further problems. Alternatively, the surplus worms can be removed and used to help repopulate another bin.

Some composters put a crumpled empty compost bag in the top of the bin to provide a worm resting place away from the hot compost.

CHAPTER 9

COMPOST ACTIVATORS

Most compost activators increase the nitrogen, phosphorus and potassium (N-P-K) levels of the composting materials or introduce strains of micro-organisms to break down the organic matter. They are variously described as compost activators, compost accelerators, compost inoculators and compost makers. The terms are more or less interchangeable. It is not necessary to add purchased activators to the compost bin if the C:N ratio is correct, but green plants or manures (natural activators) may be routinely added as an organic activator layer when composting unsorted garden waste without separating into green and brown layers. There are other substances that can be added to compost, including limestone and dolomite.

Natural activators include tender green plants that decompose quickly, manures, powdered products, coffee grounds and urine. They offer a viable solution to one of the problems encountered in managing vegetable garden and allotment bins, which is a shortage of greens from crops during certain parts of the year. This makes the use of additional greens such as comfrey or manure beneficial, and activator layers can be incorporated into the structure when the heap is being made. In home composting where kitchen waste is available throughout the year, this is less likely to be a problem.

If a heap or bin does not start decomposing, or is slow in getting going, it is likely to be due to a poor C:N balance, with the plant material containing insufficient nitrogen. In this case, the addition of an organic or artificial activator may be indicated.

Using Activators in a Layered Bin or Heap

If the compost bin or heap is of a good size (at least a cubic metre), and the organic materials have been layered alternately with greens and browns (see Chapter 7), so that the C:N ratio is correct, it should not be necessary to adjust the green:brown ratio by using additional activators as nitrogen-rich materials are already included. The same applies if the greens and browns have been measured and mixed prior to building the heap or filling the bin.

If, however, a garden bin is being used where the garden waste is added without being separated into greens and browns, the composting process may be assisted by the insertion of a layer of natural activator after every 15cm (6in) layer of garden waste. This technique is particularly helpful when community composting on an allotment as plot-holders are likely to be inconsistent in sorting their waste before leaving

Any green that decomposes quickly will act as an activator. When building a heap in the summer, grass cuttings are usually available and make a useful activator layer.

Young nettles are a readily available natural activator. A small patch can be kept and harvested every few weeks. They can also be used to make a liquid feed.

it in the reception bins. Although most of the waste will consist of greens, many of them may be very dry or hard (for example, brassica stalks).

A natural activator layer would normally consist of organic material that is readily available to allotment plot-holders or country gardeners – farmyard manure, comfrey, nettles, grass cuttings – or, for those near to the coast, seaweed. The urban composter may have ready access to used coffee grounds from local cafés. Where natural activators are not readily available, they may be purchased from the garden centre, or online, in the form of fish, blood, seaweed or pelleted chicken manure. All of these can be sprinkled onto the compost to form a thin layer.

'Natural' Activators

Green Plants

Any tender plants that are fast to decompose – for example, chopped comfrey, nettles, clover, a thin layer of fresh grass clippings – will make a good activator. Alfalfa can also be used.

Manures

Manure from chickens, cows, horses, rabbits or pigs, or less common farm animals such as alpaca, should

Older nettles can also be used but are best cut into short lengths. It is advisable to wear hand and arm protection when collecting the plants.

As with nettles, the young leaves of comfrey make the best activator, but leaves from mature plants can be used if they are cut into small pieces. Some of the plants should be left alone to flower for the bees.

The bee-friendly comfrey plant in flower.

Comfrey about to be cut to size with garden shears to provide an activator layer on the heap. Long-handled shears avoid the need for bending.

While cow manure makes a good activator it is used less often than in the past. Ideally it should be matured in a separate pile or bin before being used in composting.

ideally be matured for a year before being incorporated into the bin. They should be added in as a thin layer as possible but sometimes cow manure will be in lumps that are difficult to break up.

As a form of quality control, it is a good idea to mix the manure with soil and sow radish seeds to check for the possible presence of herbicides, which would inhibit plant growth. Some manures are available as dry products or as pellets.

Coffee Grounds and Waste

Coffee grounds can be added as an activator layer or to cold-composting systems as they become available. Many cafés will provide coffee waste free of charge. Coffee grounds can be mixed with equal parts of grass to make a green layer when preparing a hot compost bin or smaller amounts can be added as available.

Matured cow manure layered in a pallet bin.

Coffee grounds layered in a pallet bin.

Human Urine

Composters may add their own urine, diluted 1:4–1:10, to the compost heap where the compost is dry, to help speed up decomposition.

Seaweed

Seaweed contains plant nutrients, trace elements, growth hormones and other nutrients, and is particularly rich in iodine and calcium. It is also available commercially both dried and as a liquid. Small quantities of seaweed can be added directly to the bin.

If added as a separate green layer it should be shredded or chopped to 2.5–5cm (1–2in) and will decompose in a few weeks compared with six months or more for uncut fronds.

If considering collecting seaweed it must be noted that many countries have laws to protect the marine environment and it is likely that these will cover the harvesting of seaweed.

Powdered Natural Products

Blood and bonemeal and alfalfa have traditionally been sold in powder form as activators to scatter on kitchen and garden waste. They are both generally effective and certainly easier to handle than manure activators, but there is some debate as to the value of some commercially available activators. However, where a commercially available activator is being used and good compost is being produced, it is fine to continue with it. It might be worth trying a free natural product too.

Soil or Compost

Thin layers of compost or soil can also be used to provide additional microbes to help decompose the organic material. A thicker layer of soil used to top the finished bin will reduce heat loss and conserve water.

Other Additives

Home-Made Aerated Compost Tea

Home-made aerated compost tea (ACT) (*see* Chapter 13) and compost extract can be used to help maintain moisture levels while adding fungi and bacteria to the bin. The microbes in the tea will be those found in the mature compost that was used in the

The finished bin can also be topped with soil as an activator layer.

soak. These are most likely to be mesophilic organisms, which predominate in the cold compost bin and at the beginning and end of the hot-composting process, in the temperature range of 10–40°C.

The sludge left after making plant feeds and from drowning perennial weeds can also be added.

Commercially Available Microorganism and Enzyme Activators

Some commercial compost activators contain microbes, rather than nutrients, and may be described in sales information as 'inoculators'. These products usually include blends of beneficial bacteria, fungi and enzymes. It is said that these strains accelerate the composting process and improve the quality of the finished compost by the addition of bacteria or fungi that give a boost to the activity of those already in the organic material.

The inoculant is usually mixed with water and sprayed onto the compost as the heap is made or turned. Specialist compost inoculants are available for specific purposes – for example, lignin-degrading fungi can be used on woody material to reduce significantly the time taken to produce a rich compost. The end product will be more suited to the growth of annual plants or as a more fungal-dominant compost for perennial plants.

Hydrated Lime or Dolomite

Agriculture lime has been routinely added to compost to make it more alkaline where the compost is being made using acidic materials such as pine needles. However, compost will normally become neutral or slightly alkaline in the final stages of decomposition without the addition of lime. Gypsum can be used as an alternative to calcium that does not raise the pH. If the compost is too alkaline, it will lose ammonia gas to the atmosphere, depleting the compost of nitrogen. As a general rule, it may be better to lime the soil where it is required rather than adding lime to the compost heap.

CHAPTER 10

VERMICULTURE: COMPOSTING WITH WORMS

In worm composting, also known as vermicomposting, worms are used to digest organic waste and produce worm castings, which are rich in nutrients. In vermiculture (the activity of keeping worms), the composting worms live in decaying organic matter in the upper part of the soil and manure heaps. Commonly known as brandling, manure, red, tiger or dendra worms, they should not be confused with the common earthworm, *Lumbricus terrestris*, which lives in the deeper soil. The composting worms include the species *Eisenia foetida, E. andreii* and *Dendroboana veneta*. They are fast breeders, laying an egg every 10 days under good conditions, and maturing in a few weeks.

In addition to the composting worms, small white potworms will appear in the bin. They may multiply rapidly if the conditions are favourable but will not be a problem unless they start to dominate, when they will compete for food with the composting worms. They can be removed by adding a piece of bread soaked in milk to the bin. It will be irresistible to the potworms and they should move in large numbers on to it, after which it can be removed.

Commercial Vermiculture

Vermiculture on a commercial scale can support the production of compost for landscape gardening and farming, and to make worm compost tea. The worms are used to treat waste from brewing, cotton mills, agriculture (including manure), parks, gardens and the catering trade. In addition, worms are bred for fishing bait and for sale to home composters. Most worms are sold by weight, with 1kg containing between 1600 and 2000 worms.

Large-scale vermiculture can involve the use of windrows, which provide bedding materials for the worms and act as a plentiful source of organic waste. This food supply encourages the worms to remain within the windrow. The worms can also be housed commercially in a raised bed with a solid or soil base, or a bed that is raised off the ground, with a wide mesh screen forming its base. The worms are fed by adding food to the top of the bed and the worm castings are harvested by pulling a scraping bar across the mesh at the bottom. These techniques can also be used for home wormeries.

A typical selection of composting worms and smaller potworms taken from a worm bin.

Home Vermiculture

Home vermiculture has grown in popularity in recent years as it produces compost more quickly than conventional aerobic composting – in just six weeks to three months – and can be undertaken in small spaces including a balcony or even indoors. A wormery is clean and simple to use and should be free from odours. It also provides an interesting introduction to composting for children.

About one-third of household waste is likely to be kitchen-generated organic matter, which can be composted by worms. In addition to rich compost the wormery will produce 'worm wee', leachate that can be used as a nutrient-rich organic liquid feed. It is also possible to make worm tea from the worm casts, in the same way as compost tea can be made from conventional compost (*see* Chapter 13).

Creating a wormery for the home can be done cheaply. It may be as simple as a wooden or plastic box or bin with drainage holes. The worms will need bedding and this can be as basic as moist shredded newspaper or computer paper, with autumn leaves being added to retain moisture and maintain air spaces.

A bin that is being used as a home-made wormery will need holes or mesh to provide aeration and holes or a tap in the bottom to drain off the leachate (or worm wee). If a tap is fitted a reservoir can be created using a mesh layer or plastic flowerpot stand to separate the liquid for collection. If the wormery is to be moved regularly drainage holes drilled in the bottom of the bin are more practical than having a protruding tap, which might be broken in transit.

Making a wormery can be quite simple.

Drainage holes drilled in the base. If these become blocked, they can be enlarged, and additional holes can be added if the first lot are not adequate.

Flowerpot stands are placed in the bottom of the wormery to support the drainage reservoir cover.

Worms taken from the wormery three weeks after they were introduced.

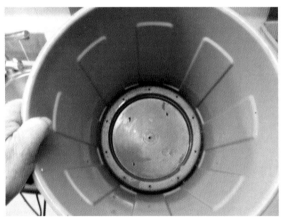

A flowerpot saucer with small holes drilled in it will create a reservoir allowing worm wee to drain from the compost.

The wormery in use after the addition of bedding and food.

Material for the Wormery

Compostable Materials

Kitchen waste suitable for worm composting includes raw vegetable peelings and fruit, including banana skins and pineapple. Cooked food, including bread, is best avoided when using a small wormery, as it may smell, although small quantities can be composted if they are buried under other waste to exclude flies. For composting significant amounts of cooked food and plate scrapings, a bokashi system is a better option (see Chapter 11) than a small domestic wormery. Coffee grounds as well as plastic-free teabags are useful additions to the wormery. Eggshells are a good source of calcium; they are best pulverised so that they are less obvious in the finished compost. Annual weeds, green leaves and cow or horse manure can also be added to an outdoor wormery.

Shredded computer paper, newspapers and cardboard make good worm bedding, as does coir; all demonstrate good moisture retention. Dried autumn leaves can also be used as bedding but will probably take longer to be consumed than paper. They are also less absorbent, so it may be necessary to add water to maintain the correct moisture level. For those who keep horses or rabbits and have a stock of hay or straw, this can be used as bedding. Both are excellent at providing air spaces, but they are not as good as paper or cardboard in terms of moisture retention.

Materials to Avoid

It is generally recommended that the following should not be added to wormeries:

- onions, shallots, leeks and garlic;
- citrus fruit;
- meat and fish;
- rice, pasta and cooked potatoes;
- dairy products;
- fat, grease and cooked meat;
- grass (produces heat when it decomposes, which may kill the worms);
- perennial weeds and diseased plant material;
- glossy paper;
- cat faeces (may carry the parasite *Toxoplasma gondii*, which can infest the human foetus);
- dog faeces, although waste from wormed, healthy and non-pregnant adult dogs can be treated in a separate dog poo wormery (*see* below) with paper or cardboard as bedding. The finished compost should not be used on the vegetable garden or in any place where children might come into contact with it.

Cooked meat may be composted but the process is slow and might attract flies. It may also create unpleasant odours if left on the surface of the bedding. Small amounts of meat and dairy products can be added, but they should be buried rather than left on the surface.

Plant seeds from fruit and vegetable scraps and perennial weeds will not be killed in a wormery and are likely to germinate when the finished compost is spread on the garden. However, this need not be a problem. Any seeds or young plants may be extracted from the finished compost and seedlings may be removed by hoeing.

The common advice is that plants in the onion family and citrus fruits should not be added to a wormery as they may increase the acidity to a level that will kill the worms. Having excessive amounts of onion in a wormery is even said to burn the skin of the worms. It is said that worms do not like the smell of the onion family, so given a choice, they will leave them uneaten until they begin to rot. It will certainly take longer for the worms to eat the dry outer layer of onions. However, many composters do add onions, shallots, leeks and garlic to their wormeries, either cooked or in small amounts, and find that these materials in moderation do not generally cause problems. When adding more acidic materials, the pH should be checked regularly and lime added, as necessary, to keep the contents at or near pH 7.

On balance, onion skins and scraps are best treated in a bokashi bin or added to a traditional compost bin. They will not negatively affect the composting microbes present in the bin, but there is another factor to consider, which is that their odour may attract pests and unwelcome wildlife. Whichever method is used, they are best cut into small pieces before being added so that they break down more quickly. Adding shredded paper, newspaper and cardboard may help control the onion smell and reduce the risk of it attracting pests.

The situation is similar with citrus fruit, which contains limonene, a chemical that is toxic to worms. The advice is generally that citrus should not be added to a wormery but dry citrus skins in reasonable amounts do not appear to have a significant effect on the acidity of the bin or on the worms, as they tend to leave them alone until they start to decompose.

A small amount of grit should be added to the wormery to help the worms break up food in their gizzard. Pulverised eggshells are often used, but the crushed oyster shells that are often given to chickens are also suitable, as is vermiculite. Garden soil can also be used. Under favourable conditions, the compost will be ready to harvest in three to five months.

Worm Bedding

Alongside compostable waste, the right bedding for the worms is important to the success of a wormery. The worms will eventually eat the bedding, but it also provides them with insulation and a source of carbon and assists with moisture retention. Bedding also allows the movement of air through the medium and gives the composter a place to bury the food for the worms. Suitable materials for bedding include shredded computer paper, shredded or torn-up newspaper, cardboard, coir, peat moss, leaf mould or woodchip.

Used bedding from small animals such as rabbits, guinea pigs and mice can be added to the wormery (along with any faeces), provided the pet bedding material is suitable for the worms. Any product that is sold as being for small animals should be safe to use. Sawdust can also be added but it will be slow to break down and should not be derived from treated timber. Composted

Shredded paper can be used as bedding for the worms.

cow or horse manure can be used as bedding in outdoor wormeries, but it is likely to produce an unpleasant odour during the initial stages. Fresh manure should not be used as it may heat up as it decomposes and kill the worms. Chicken manure and droppings from other birds have a high ammonia content and are best left to age or added to the conventional compost bin.

Contained Wormeries

While it is relatively easy to make a home-made wormery from wood or repurposed plastic bins, the majority of domestic wormeries are purchased from a worm farm or commercial supplier of composting equipment.

Single-Chamber Wormery or All-in-One Wormery

The simplest commercial style of home wormery is a single container with holes or a reservoir at the base with a tap to allow drainage and collection of the worm wee.

Different types of wormery (left to right): two stacking wormeries; Original Organics single-chamber wormery; Can-O-Worms stacking wormery; dog poo wormery.

Harvesting a single-chamber wormery requires a little more effort than emptying a stacking wormery, and this can be a factor when choosing a system. Composting worms normally live in the top layer of the compost, just below the food waste. It is therefore a simple job to remove the food waste and the top 20–30cm (8–12in) layer of compost, which will contain most of the worms, and save that layer to be returned to the empty wormery later. The rest of the contents are tipped on to a plastic sheet. The worms will be attracted to the cones of compost on the sheet, making it easy to collect them and put them back in the wormery. Alternatively, the compost can be spread out on the plastic sheet and parts covered with damp newspaper. The worms will move under the paper to get out of the light and can then be collected. The rest of the finished compost can be harvested, while uncomposted material and the worms are returned to the container, to restart the composting cycle.

If the wormery has a drainage tap it is best mounted on a stand to make it easier to drain off the worm wee. There are a range of sizes available to suit different needs, ranging from small bins for single people to large wheelie bins.

The single-chamber wormery from Original Organics should produce worm wee in about 10 weeks and a good yield of compost every eight to 12 months.

Stacking or Multi-Tray Wormery

This type of wormery consists of a reservoir, usually on legs or supported off the ground, to collect the worm wee and two or more trays that stack one above the

Can-O-Worms stacking wormery, comprising a reservoir with a tap and two trays.

Urbalive modern stacking wormery.

other. The worms and kitchen waste are placed in the first tray to start the wormery. When this is nearly full the second composting tray is added. A small amount of the compost from the bottom tray is added to the new one, so that the worms have something familiar to move into. Waste food is added to the new tray in the

Stacking wormery using a stand similar to those on the stacking units.

The top tray of a stacking wormery showing the contents before new food and bedding are added.

The central tray with some worms and slugs visible on the surface along with some pumpkin seeds (which may go on to germinate later when the compost is spread).

The bottom tray, with some worms still present. Most have followed the food up to the central and top trays.

A patio wormery with lid.

normal way. When this tray is full, the process is repeated with the next tray and subsequent trays. By the time the third or fourth tray is full, most of the worms will have left the first tray and the compost can be harvested.

It is easy to harvest the compost from stacking wormeries as the worms will work their way up to the top trays in search of food. The bottom tray containing the completed compost can then be removed, emptied and put back ready on the top of the wormery.

There are a number of different types of stacking wormery, including patio wormeries and home-made wormeries using stacking boxes.

A patio wormery with herbs growing in the top.

A home-made stacking wormery. The bottom reservoir unit is fitted with a drainage tap.

Indoor Wormeries

Many wormeries are suitable for use indoors, where they will not be exposed to wide fluctuations in temperature or damage by sunlight. Unless they are fitted with a reservoir and drainage tap, they are probably better suited to an outhouse.

In addition to plastic bins, a 30-litre stainless steel wormery is available specifically for indoor use by a family of two or three. It will stand on a worktop in a kitchen or utility room and fit under the over-bench cupboards, but may need to be moved when adding food.

A small indoor wormery suitable for a school biology lab, garden shed or outbuilding.

An indoor stainless-steel wormery that contains a reservoir, has a clip-on lid, and is easily cleaned.

Garden Wormeries

Raised Worm Beds

Using a normal raised bed as a worm bed will provide one of the simplest methods of breeding worms in the garden. It will be easy to maintain and if made using a second-hand pallet will have the additional advantage of being cheap, foldable and stackable. Ideally the wormery should be in a shady location so that it is not dried out or overheated by the summer sun. It is recommended to line the bottom of the bed with corrugated cardboard.

The worms will need to be separated from the compost when it is harvested. Prior to harvesting, the contents of the raised bed can be pushed or shovelled to one side and fresh bedding placed in the space made available. If the worms' food is added to the new bedding for a period of about a month, most of the worms will have moved to the new feeding grounds and the abandoned compost can be allowed to mature. It can then be harvested and replaced with fresh bedding.

Dug-In Worm Beds

One variation on the raised bed is a wormery dug or buried in the ground. A pit about the depth of the height of a raised bed is dug, and the sides lined with boards, bricks or blocks. Alternatively, a pallet collar can be let into the ground. Layers of moistened shredded paper make excellent bedding for this type of wormery. The food scraps should be buried in the bedding to protect them from vermin.

Commercially available dug-in wormeries, such as the Subpod, are best used in a raised bed. These will not only produce worm compost but also nutrients that will feed the soil.

A Subpod in-ground wormery dug into a raised bed. The worms can leave and return to the wormery as they please.

The Subpod wormery ready to receive fresh food and bedding. Normally, one side would be topped up at a time.

Operating a Wormery

Starting a Wormery

When a new wormery is purchased, it will normally be supplied with a starter kit containing bedding, such as coir blocks. This will normally require soaking in a bucket of warm water for about 30 minutes before being squeezed to the consistency of a wrung-out sponge and added to the wormery. If making a home-made wormery, or bringing an existing one back into use, an 8–10cm (3.25–4in) layer of moist compost (with the consistency of a wrung-out sponge) can be used as the initial bedding material.

The worms may be supplied with a commercially available wormery, purchased from a worm farm, or taken from an existing wormery or manure heap. Some sources recommend adding the worms to the wormery and then leaving them to settle but others suggest adding a layer of kitchen waste at this stage. Adding used compost or garden soil to the bedding will encourage the worms to settle otherwise they might decide to try to escape from the wormery during the first couple of nights.

Once the worms have had a chance to make themselves properly at home they should be fed little and often, but they will need to be well established first. People often kill the worms in their newly established wormery by overfeeding them. The best procedure is to leave the worms undisturbed for a week or two so that they can settle down, with just a small amount of the worm food supplied with the wormery being added once a week. This should be followed by a small handful of kitchen food waste three or four times a week. It is better to chop or tear the food into small pieces so that it starts to rot and can be eaten more quickly.

Once the worms are eating, the food can either be buried, about 3 to 5cm (1 to 2in) deep, in the bedding material or compost to create feeding pockets, or placed on top of the compost. Placing the food on the compost makes it easier to monitor whether the worms are eating it and helps avoid overfeeding. Moist cardboard or shredded paper or other suitable material can be added to provide bedding and as a carbon source each time the worms are fed. In turn, the organic material can be covered with cardboard cut to fit the wormery to help maintain the moisture level.

Deciding how much to feed the worms is in practice a matter of trial and error. Depending on their species, worms can eat between one-half and the whole of their body weight every day so if the wormery was started by buying 1kg of worms they should be fed about 0.5kg of food waste per day, or 3.5kg a week. As the worms can double in numbers every 60 to 90 days, the food should be gradually increased. However, observation provides the most reliable method of assessing the food requirements, using the tried and tested method of looking to see how much they have eaten and adding fresh food when required. Providing grit will help the worms digest the food – crushed eggshells are a good source for this.

Once the wormery is established it can be left without attention for three or four weeks, so it will not be necessary for the composter to take the worms away on holiday with them. However, they will continue to produce worm wee, so the reservoir tap should be left open over a tray or bottle to prevent the compost becoming waterlogged.

Pumpkins in wormeries following a 'Pumpkin Smash' event.

Managing a Wormery

As with conventional composting, the key environmental actors in a wormery are temperature, ventilation, moisture content, pH level and the space available for the colony to expand, together with sufficient food to support a positive growth rate. These are discussed in general terms in Chapter 3, but specific requirements for vermiculture are given below.

Moisture

Composting worms like a moist but not waterlogged environment. They do not have lungs but 'breathe' through their skin, which must be kept moist. Covering the compost in the top tray of the wormery with cardboard will help retain the moisture. To avoid waterlogging in a plastic wormery, it is important to see that any drainage holes are kept clear and that the reservoir for the worm wee is drained regularly, otherwise the worms might 'drown'. If the wormery is being left alone for a week or so, the drainage tap should be open all the time, so that the wee can drain into a container. Adding dry bedding every couple of weeks will also help prevent waterlogging.

pH

Composting worms prefer an approximately neutral pH of 6.5–7. This can be easily checked using a pH meter. If it is too acidic, the worms may try to escape from the unfavourable conditions and be found in large numbers on the lid. It this occurs, the pH can be adjusted by adding crushed limestone to the worm bedding. This can be obtained from most suppliers of wormeries. Hydrated lime should not be used as it will kill the worms. Crushed eggshells may also be used instead of lime. They can be dried by heating in an oven, ground to a fine powder with a pestle and mortar and then sprinkled on the wormery. This will not only help to adjust the pH, but also provide grit, which the worms need in order to digest their food more easily.

Temperature

Worms normally live in the soil and like moist, warm conditions within a temperature range of about

18–25°C. Some variation of temperature can be tolerated but unfavourable conditions will adversely affect the activity of the worms. When the temperature in a wormery starts to drop below 15°C, the worms will reproduce less readily. If it continues to drop, they will go into survival mode; below 4 degrees, they will start to die off. Similarly, if the temperature rises over 25°C, the worms will start to eat and reproduce less; at a slightly higher temperature, they will either try to escape en masse or start to die. For this reason, the wormery should be kept out of direct sunlight or shaded in the summer. A plentiful supply of moist shredded newspaper bedding and corrugated cardboard in the wormery will provide insulation, create air pockets and protect from freezing during the winter. If kept moist, it will also help prevent overheating during the summer.

Wormeries can be kept successfully outdoors in the UK, but they may need to be moved into a shed or garage during the winter, and perhaps during the hottest part of the summer. Where this is not possible, wrapping in a triple layer of bubble wrap will help protect a wormery against freezing temperatures. A removable bubble wrap lid should be provided and the air vents to the wormery checked to ensure that they are not obstructed. During the winter months the

In the UK a triple layer of bubble wrap should provide sufficient insulation for the worms to survive outdoors during a normal winter.

worms will eat less due to the lower temperature, and break down their food much more slowly, so it is important to monitor the food levels to avoid over-feeding during this period.

Outdoor wormeries in the snow. Normally, they are protected from the winter weather by wrapping in bubble wrap, but these are wrapped in loft insulation in plastic bags.

Ventilation

Worms 'breathe' through their skin and need a constant supply of oxygen, so ventilation is vital. It also helps prevent the wormery smelling. A regular supply of fresh bedding should be provided to create air pockets within the bin. Ideally, about 20–30% of the bin contents should be browns – cardboard, shredded paper or wood chips – to provide sufficient space for air to circulate. If worms are found on the lid of the wormery it may well be the case that there is insufficient oxygen in the bedding and conditions have become anaerobic. Providing additional bedding and gently mixing the contents should introduce more air. Any ventilation holes or mesh should be checked and cleaned if necessary.

Worm Wee

Worm wee or 'worm juice' is the leachate that has drained from the food, bedding and worms in a wormery and through the vermicomposted material. It should not be confused with worm tea, which is made by suspending or soaking mature worm compost in water and extracting the nutrients and microorganisms. When making aerated worm tea (AWT) (see Chapter 13), the water is aerated during the process so that it contains high levels of oxygen, which encourages microbial growth.

Worm wee will have passed through the worm and the food being composted and the worm compost in its various stages. It will contain nutrients but, as the liquid will also have passed through decomposing food material, it may carry some unwanted and mainly anaerobic microbes. Oxygenating it with an aquarium or compost tea pump encourages the growth of aerobes at the expense of the anaerobes. However, the worm wee is usually simply diluted fresh from the wormery and used untreated. The advice is that if it smells unpleasant, it should not be used in this way. If it is does smell, the wormery should be checked as this suggests that all is not well with the worms or composting process. In most cases, though, it will be safe to use and should be available in significant quantities as it is continuously collected in the wormery reservoir.

The chemical content of the worm wee will vary considerably but it has been found to contain calcium, magnesium, nitrogen (mostly as nitrate), phosphorus, potassium and sodium, plus small amounts of boron, copper, iron, manganese, molybdenum and zinc.

The worm wee should be drained off regularly and diluted 1:10 in rainwater or to the colour of weak tea and used around plants or on the soil.

Dog and Cat Faeces

The question is often asked as to whether a wormery can be used to produce compost from poo from domestic pets. The answer is that is possible, but with some significant reservations: it is not recommended to treat cat poo in this way and precautions are certainly necessary when treating dog poo.

The main problem with composting any manure is the need to kill any pathogenic bacteria and parasites that are present. In the case of cat poo, this means the protozoal parasite *Toxoplasma gondii*, which causes human toxoplasmosis. Although the illness usually gives rise to only mild symptoms, it can be extremely serious in individuals whose immunity is compromised, including pregnant women and their unborn child, babies and young children, the elderly and the immunosuppressed (for example, those receiving anti-cancer treatment). In the high-risk groups, toxoplasmosis can be associated with severe illness and devastating outcomes including encephalitis, abortion, stillbirth, birth defects and other problems affecting the nervous system and eyes.

Dog poo can also carry parasites and the main risk is associated with a roundworm *Toxocara canis*. If the eggs are ingested by humans, the larvae will migrate and encyst in the soft tissues. If they settle in the eye, this can result in blindness. The most vulnerable group is young children, who might eat contaminated soil, but there is a small risk of ingestion from contaminated vegetables.

A wormery used solely to process faeces from adult dogs that have been regularly wormed, with composting ceasing during pregnancy, presents an acceptable risk if good hygiene procedures are followed and the compost is used only on flower gardens in an area that is not accessible to young children. Subject to these

A single-chamber dog poo wormery. Cardboard and shredded paper are used to provide bedding and a carbon source for the worms.

controls, dog poo wormeries offer an effective means of dealing with the waste without mess, fuss or smell. Although any wormery can be used to compost dog poo, it is advisable to use a separate unit just for dog's faeces and not to compost normal kitchen food waste at the same time. Cardboard and shredded paper can be used as bedding and as a carbon source.

A single-chamber wormery can be used for this purpose, but this will involve the owner being faced with a decomposing pile of poo every time they want to harvest the compost. With a stacking wormery of three or more trays with a lid, drainage sump and stand, harvesting will be easier and more pleasant, as the bottom tray will contain compost with no identifiable faeces or smell. It should be used for dog poo in the same way as for normal waste, with the faeces being deposited in the lowest tray first. Once that has been filled with faeces and paper or cardboard, the upper trays are brought into use while the composting process is completed in the lower tray.

The compost (worm castings) can be harvested as the worms move to the upper layers. The bottom sump collects the worm wee, which can be diluted 1:10 and used as a fertiliser on the flower garden.

The bins should not smell when in use provided the mix is right, and the finished compost cannot be distinguished from compost made from garden or kitchen waste. As a general guide, a wormery with two composting trays is suitable for a household with a small dog, three composting trays will be adequate for a medium-sized dog or two small dogs, and four trays will serve a large dog (or two medium dogs). Larger wheelie-bin type wormeries are available that will deal with faeces from up to eight large or 15 small dogs.

CHAPTER 11

BOKASHI FERMENTATION

Bokashi is associated with northeast and central Asia and probably originated in Japan or Korea, where early farmers would bury their waste, allow soil microorganisms to ferment the material and then mix that material with soil to use in growing crops. The process involves anaerobic fermentation, unlike the aerobic decomposition by microorganisms that occurs in conventional aerobic composting. Fermentation is a preservation process during which oxygen is eliminated, lowering the pH, and preserving the organic material being processed. This is why at the end of the pre-composting process it has changed little in appearance.

Modern bokashi was developed in Japan and requires the addition of what are known as effective microorganisms (EM). This is a mixture of lactic-acid-producing bacteria such as *Lactobacillus* spp., phototrophic bacteria such as *Rhodopseudomonas* spp., and yeasts such as *Saccharomyces* spp.

Using a bokashi system and EM is environmentally friendly as it does not generate heat, which results in less loss of organic matter and lower carbon dioxide emissions than aerobic composting. It also creates a greater microbial diversity and aids the build-up of humus, leading to improved moisture retention and greater carbon sequestration in the soil.

Bokashi is used by farmers, horticulturalists, fruit and wine growers and riding schools, who use their

Entry-level bokashi bins are sometimes available in the UK as part of an offer from local councils, to encourage food composting.

carbon-rich waste material, such as straw, grape marc and food waste, together with nitrogen-rich material such as effluent and appropriate EM, to produce an environmentally friendly soil enhancer. The EM additive used in home composting and most commercial

Table 11.1 Kitchen and garden waste that can be treated in the bokashi bin

Food waste (raw and cooked)	
Suitable	Bread, cakes, cheese, coffee grounds, chaff and filters, dairy products, fish, fresh fruit (including citrus), grains, meat, onions, pasta, prepared foods, rice, salads, teabags, vegetables.
Add with care	Mouldy or rotten food may introduce undesirable fungi. With bones, the fermentation process will remove meat and potential pathogenic microorganisms, and the bones can then be crushed and composted. Materials such as eggshells and bones will also be decomposed but they will take much longer to break down and will be visible in the pre-compost when it is added to the compost bin or buried with the rest of the pre-compost, or returned to the bokashi bin for further treatment.
Unsuitable	Liquids, for example, water, milk or fruit juice, unless absorbed by bread or kitchen towel.
Garden waste (in windrows, not indoor bins)	
Suitable	Organic garden waste and 'sub-standard' vegetables, grass, windfalls, leaf waste, woodchip, manure.

systems is normally purchased but it can be made on site using bran or rice bran as a medium.

While commercial-scale composting is beyond the scope of this book it is worth considering the systems used, as they can be reduced in size and used to deal with a range of materials:

- garden waste from larger gardens, estates and municipal growers;
- 'sub-standard' vegetables from horticultural growers;
- peelings from vegetable preparation;
- windfalls and prunings from fruit growers;
- leaf waste and wood chips from landscape gardeners;
- manure from stables and cattle slurry from smallholdings; and
- garden waste from community gardens and allotments.

Bokashi Composting in Windrows

In most large-scale bokashi systems, the waste and EM are formed into windrows using organic matter to give a C:N ratio of about 1:20, with 25–50% dry matter. In one technique an amount of waste being composted is mixed with the same amount of sawdust or paper. A quantity of rock phosphate (2kg) and of elemental sulphur (200g) can also be added. All the ingredients are combined thoroughly with 3–5 litres of EM being added to the final mix. The windrow

is then covered with a plastic sheet to exclude air and rainwater, reducing leachate loss from the heap. The edges of the sheet are buried and weighed down with soil.

In addition to the EM, other additives may be used to assist the process. One commercial system developed by Agriton uses seashell grit as a source of calcium carbonate, to help regulate the pH, and clay minerals to bind minerals and nutrients in the windrow, in addition to Actiferm or Microferm, ready-to-use EM suspensions of bacteria, fungi, yeast and actinomycetes. While there is a cost involved in purchasing the necessary additives, it will be lower than the expense of transporting waste off-site and buying fertiliser that could be produced from the green waste.

The system used in agriculture can be scaled down to suit allotments or large gardens.

A mechanical means of turning will make mixing the materials much easier, but even when mixing with a fork, windrows approximately 3m wide and 1m high can be used. The windrow should ideally have straight sides and a flat top as this enables a better fit and air exclusion when it is covered with plastic sheet. If turning and mixing are to be done by hand, it is a good idea to invite friends to assist.

To provide a measure of the finished size of the windrow it can be helpful to spread the unmixed organic materials in a row of the desired height and width to the side of the final windrow position and then work along the row giving it a preliminary turn to mix the materials. The top section is then removed and mixed to form base layer of the final windrow alongside the first row.

In a large-scale system, each tonne of organic material will require the addition of 12kg of Aegir seaside lime, 12kg of Edasil clay and 2 litres of EM Actiferm. Much smaller windrows can also be used, though. The model on the Leicester Allotments composting demonstration site, for example, is only about 2 metres (6.5ft) long. A small windrow such as this can be built directly on top of a plastic sheet laid on the ground. The sheet can then be pulled over the sides of the windrow and sealed, like pastry round a sausage roll. This prevents the loss of any leachate, retaining all the goodness in the finished compost.

Bokashi windrow with the wrapping removed to show the fermented garden waste after a few weeks.

Making a small bokashi windrow on the allotment. It is being constructed on a large plastic sheet, which will be wrapped around it to exclude air.

A small bokashi windrow. Wrapping it completely in plastic means that the leachate will be absorbed rather than draining into the soil.

Two-thirds of the additives (lime and clay) are added along the top of the base level. Working along the windrow from one end, the additives are turned into the windrow. The diluted liquid EM (Actiferm) is added using a watering can. The other third of the solid additives are mixed with the remaining organic material and put on top of the base row to complete the windrow. The rest of the diluted EM liquid is added.

The sides of the windrow should be built as vertical as possible to add weight and the whole structure packed down to remove air pockets. In the case of a conventional windrow where the leachate is allowed to drain into the soil, a small gully about a spit deep (approximately the length of the blade of a spade) is dug round the compacted windrow. The windrow is then covered with two plastic sheets, the ends of which are buried in the gullies. The first sheet excludes air to create anaerobic conditions while the second sheet protects the first against mechanical damage.

In anaerobic windrow composting the windrows are not turned during the process, as they are in aerobic composting. The compost is produced relatively quickly – about eight weeks or a little longer. The levels of energy and nutrients in the resultant compost are higher than those found in aerobic compost as little heat is generated by the anaerobic process.

The number of windrows required for continuous composting will depend on the size of the operation, the rate at which waste is produced and the storage space available for waste awaiting treatment. If required, the initial windrow can be expanded by adding fresh material at one end and harvesting the finished product from the other end by opening just enough of the plastic sheet. If this technique is to be used, the sheet used to cover the windrow should be cut accordingly, with extra length at one end left empty and folded up when the windrow is started. This can then be used later, avoiding the need to make any joints as new material is added.

Leachate, also known as 'bokashi tea' and containing nutrients, proteins and lactic acid, may be produced in significant quantities – about 10% of the input by weight. It is normally collected for use by direct application to the soil or it can be left to drain into the soil under the windrow. In garden windrows, leachate might be collected by drainage from a sloping concrete base into a bucket sunk into the ground or by absorption into a base layer of cardboard or biochar (*see* Chapter 1). If a fermentation vessel is used, the bokashi tea is collected in a reservoir from which it can be run off for use.

Bokashi Composting in Bins

Dealing with Kitchen Waste

It is often said that cooked food waste cannot be home composted, but this statement needs qualification. In fact, cooked food waste can be composted aerobically if a hot-composting bin is used, but suitable systems tend to be relatively expensive. Food waste can also be buried directly in the garden in a trench or post hole, but this involves digging and keeping track of pits or trenches over the garden, and may attract vermin.

Bokashi anaerobic composting offers an alternative approach in which waste (including cooked food waste) is fermented in a sealed airtight container to produce pre-compost, which can then be added to a conventional compost bin or wormery or buried directly in the soil. The bokashi stage of the process will take about 30 days.

Domestic bins for bokashi composting are available in a range of sizes: for example, 15 litres, 18 litres, 23 litres, 27 litres, 30 litres (stainless). A pair of

The Hozelock bokashi bin has a contrasting rubberised lid, which is easier to fit than a rigid one.

Rather than the usual bran, the Urban Composter bokashi system uses a citrus-scented spray that contains the effective microorganisms (EM).

bins are normally used so that, when the first bin has been filled and is fermenting, a second bin is available to take the current waste. If two bins are insufficient, it is probably better to use a third than to increase the bin size.

Larger bokashi bins are available for commercial use and can be set up in banks of six or seven for medium- to larger-scale operations at cafés, restaurants, small businesses and nurseries.

Advantages of Bokashi

There are three main advantages of bokashi over home closed-vessel hot-composting systems:
* lower initial cost;
* waste can be added to a bokashi bin indoors straight from the plate or kitchen board, eliminating the need for a kitchen caddy; and
* it is simple and does not involve balancing greens and browns. The waste is simply added to the bin and compressed to remove air, the bokashi bran is added and the bin is sealed.

A commercially available domestic bokashi bin normally consists of a plastic bin with carry handle, airtight lid and tap. It has an inner drain tray to allow separation of the food scraps and liquid produced by the system and to prevent the solid material blocking the drainage tap. It will often come with a measuring scoop, a tool for compressing the organic material and even a liquid drain cup.

Use of a bokashi bin will require the regular purchase of bokashi bran but this is relatively low cost, and the composter can make their own. The microorganisms are introduced by spreading bokashi bran thinly on the base of the bucket before adding the first layer of food waste. This is most helpful when the system being used does not include a drainage tap. The waste is cut into lengths of 3–4cm (1–1.5in), to enable the microorganisms to ferment the food effectively, and added in layers about 3–4cm thick. If possible, the food waste should be added to the bin when fresh. A measure or tablespoon of bokashi bran is then scattered on top of each layer of waste food. Air pockets are removed by compression using the tool provided or a potato masher that is kept for the purpose.

The layering process is repeated as material becomes available, alternating food waste with bran, remembering to seal the bucket each time to exclude the air. Once the bucket is full, the organic material should be covered with cardboard, newspaper or plastic to exclude air and the lid closed to start the process. (A sheet or two of newspaper can be placed in the bottom of the bucket to absorb the liquid, but the bokashi system is not recommended as a means of composting significant amounts of card or paper. Instead, these should be added to a conventional compost bin or recycled.) The full bokashi bin is left closed and undisturbed for two weeks or more, with the 'juice' being drained off every couple of days.

Using Two Bins

In order to work effectively, the system requires the use of two bokashi bins. The bin in current use is normally kept in the kitchen or utility room so that plate scrapings and other food waste can be added directly to it. Once full, the bin is set aside for two weeks, and the second bin is brought into use. The full bin containing the fermenting pre-compost can be housed in a garage, shed or even in a garden storage box to

Composters may use a domestic bokashi bin to produce pre-compost from cooked food waste.

Bokashi bran being added to food waste and coffee filters.

Food with a bran layer sprinkled on the surface.

The compressed waste and bran about to be covered as a further measure to exclude air.

Compressing the kitchen waste and bran to exclude air helps create anaerobic conditions.

During the time it takes to fill the bin with food waste it should be drained regularly.

A bokashi bin that is almost full; it will soon be ready to be rested for 14 days.

protect it from the rain, sun and frost. If conditions do turn colder, the fermentation process will slow down, so it should be left to digest for a longer period (perhaps three weeks or more instead of two).

Bokashi Tea or Juice

During the fermenting process, the bin will produce a liquid known as bokashi tea or juice, which needs to be drained off every two to three days. It will leach out during the initial stage, while the food waste is being added, especially if juicy fruit and vegetables are being treated in small amounts and it is taking some time to fill the bin. More juice will also be produced when the

Bokashi liquid ('juice') being drained from the bin.

bin is set aside during the fermentation period. It will be a reddish, orangey colour with a slightly fruity or vinegary smell. There may be a thin white coating on the surface or white fungal threads floating in the liquid. If it is drained off every other day, it should be prevented from turning sour and smelling unpleasant.

The juice contains microorganisms from the food waste. The large numbers of active microbes living in it when it is fresh are said to make it an excellent compost activator or enhancer. If it is diluted before being added to a heap or bin, it will both activate and moisten the contents during dry periods. This is especially useful with plastic bins.

Containing nitrogen, phosphorus and potassium, plus other nutrients (which may include chlorine, iron, zinc, boron and manganese), bokashi juice is also a good liquid feed and soil enhancer. The juice is diluted 1:100 with water and sprayed or watered onto bare soil using a watering can fitted with a rose. It is acidic, so it should not be allowed to come into contact with any foliage at this concentration. However, diluted at a ratio of 1:500, it may be used as a foliar spray, after testing on a single leaf.

Concentrated bokashi juice can also be run off from the bin and poured undiluted down the kitchen and bathroom sink, and the toilet. The acidity will help prevent algae growth and reduce odour.

Fungal Mould

It is quite normal for a white mould to grow on the fermenting material. As the fermentation is an anaerobic process, the bin should be opened only when fresh material is being added. The growth of a green mould is a sign that there might be a problem, possibly inadequate fermentation. During the early stages of green mould growth, the situation may be rectified by adding more bokashi bran and setting the bin aside to allow time for fermentation to recommence. However, if the green mould is extensive, the bin should be emptied and the mouldy waste bagged and sent to landfill.

White mould may grow on the surface of the fermenting material during the resting period.

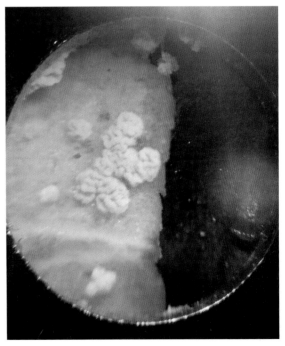

Magnified mould on bokashi contents.

A second type of mould growing during the fermentation period.

Using the Pre-Compost

After two or three weeks of fermentation in the sealed bokashi bin the pre-compost will have changed very little in appearance, but the EM organisms will have enabled microorganisms to break it down quickly.

Adding to a Compost Bin

The pre-compost can be added to an active compost bin as the final stage in the process. Finishing the process by composting achieves the original objective of converting cooked food waste to a form that can be used as a soil improver at home without attracting vermin. Many bokashi enthusiasts like to add the pre-compost directly to the soil, but this may not be practical for someone who has limited space and no room for a trench or for post-hole composting.

Adding the bokashi pre-compost to an aerobic composting bin or wormery will mean that the anaerobes responsible for fermenting the waste will be replaced by aerobic microbes. The pre-compost is normally added to a partially filled working compost bin. If a plastic cone-shaped 'Dalek' bin is being used to cold compost the normal household and garden waste, the contents should be aerated when the bokashi pre-compost is added. It is mixed with a couple of spadefuls of fresh soil or compost and the upper layers of the bin are turned so that the pre-compost is well mixed with the existing ingredients and buried. If using a New Zealand bin, where the contents are not turned, the pre-compost is mixed

with soil before being added as a layer to the bin. If hot composting and turning the contents only for the first month, the pre-compost can be added as a separate layer followed by a soil layer and then alternative layers of greens and browns.

Adding the Pre-Compost to a Wormery

Bokashi pre-compost can be added to a wormery with care in relatively small amounts over several days, together with additional browns, such as shredded paper, to maintain the C:N ratio. The pH should be checked, and lime added if the wormery bedding becomes acidic.

Once the worms have adjusted to the new material, they process it more quickly than material that has not be pre-treated.

Trench Composting

The pre-compost can be buried in a hole (as in post-hole composting), but it is preferable to use the trench-composting method, digging a 30cm (12in) deep trench to bury the product (often with the addition of uncooked kitchen waste) and covering it with soil.

The pre-compost will be acidic, probably pH 3.5–4, but the pH will adjust to that of the soil in two or three weeks. There should not be any problem in sowing seeds on ground where bokashi pre-compost has been buried, provided the roots will not reach it for at least a couple of weeks.

If burying bokashi on its own rather than mixed with uncooked vegetable waste, the pre-compost may require two to six weeks to take on the appearance of soil, depending on the temperature and how well it is mixed.

Soil Factory for Bokashi in a Flat or Apartment

A lack of access to a garden does not mean that kitchen waste cannot be processed using the bokashi system. The pre-compost can be treated in a 'soil factory' that can be housed on a balcony or in an indoor storage area. The soil factory is simply a container into which the pre-compost is deposited to mature and complete the composting process. It can comprise a single plastic bin or stacking plastic storage boxes, which have the advantage of being easy to clean and store. A lid is not essential, but it will keep pets out of the material. It should not be airtight as the soil factory, unlike the original bokashi bin, is aerobic and needs air.

A full bokashi bin will contain 16–19 litres of waste, and the product is to be used with a soil factory. Using the normal ratio of 1 part bokashi to 2 parts soil will require a 60-litre capacity container to allow for turning the material. Two medium-sized containers are better than one large one as they may need to be moved when full, and the second can be brought into use when there is no more room in the first. The container should have drainage holes and be stood in

A bokashi soil factory. The finished bokashi being added to soil in a container (soil factory).

Finished soil from a soil factory.

a tray to collect the leachate, to avoid staining the floor or decking.

Ideally, the lower 10cm (4in) of the container should be filled with fresh good-quality soil. Newly made compost from a garden or wormery that contains a good supply of microorganisms and worms to supplement the soil will give the factory a good start. However, some say that the old soil from a pot plant or a patio container can also work, providing a way of reusing soil that becomes available when repotting plants as they grow.

The pre-compost is then added directly from the bokashi bin, covered with a 5–7.5cm (2–3in) layer of fresh soil and mixed well. This layering can be repeated until the container is full, with a top layer of about 10cm (4in) of soil. The loose-fitting lid is then put in place. If a lid is not available, the material can be covered with newspaper or even an old towel to assist with moisture retention.

The waste will take between three and 12 weeks to break down completely, depending on the temperature and the type of material. It is worth checking progress after two to four weeks. At this stage, the proportion of material recognisable as waste food will have decreased and that of 'soil' will have increased. Mixing the contents of the soil factory weekly will speed up the process. The waste breaks down more quickly when warm but it should not be allowed to get too hot (over 40°C). Decomposition slows at lower temperatures so during the winter it is best to keep the set-up indoors or to insulate it well. If it is left on a balcony the temperature should not be allowed to fall below 6°C.

Additional pre-compost can be added to top up the container at any time, provided the contents are mixed well after each addition. The same container can be reused without cleaning by leaving some soil in the bottom to mix with the next batch of bokashi pre-compost, but it is preferable to clean the container and start another soil factory.

It is worth checking the pH of the 'super soil' produced as it might be acidic. This should rectify itself if the material is left for a couple of weeks. The finished product can be used as a soil improver to top up flowerpots, in window boxes or outdoor pots or growing spaces.

CHAPTER 12

USING COMPOST

Checking for Maturity

It is important to be able to recognise when the composting process is completed. Finished compost looks dark and crumbly and has an earthy smell, and most of the organic items that were added to the bin or heap will no longer be identifiable. The texture of the compost will depend on the type of materials composted and the process. Even samples taken at random directly from a range of compost bins on the same site will vary in appearance and feel. Experience shows that home composting using kitchen waste and mown grass as the main greens, and cardboard, chicken bedding and shredded paper as the browns produces a finer, darker product than allotment bins, where the compost may contain more lumps. The lumps do not necessarily pose a problem, as most of them are easily broken up, or they can be left and used as part of a mulch. If a finer material is required, the finished compost can be sieved to separate out the more stubborn materials, such as corn cobs, wood-chip and eggshells, which may still be recognisable. The bigger pieces can be removed by hand during sieving or 'screening'.

For many home composters, the look and feel of the product, and a pleasant earthy smell, will be enough to make a decision on whether their compost is finished and ready for use. However, community sites, schools and those planning to apply the compost to the soil immediately without further storage may want to test the material, to check its maturity. This can be done either by carrying out the three-day bag test (*see* Chapter 7) or a simple germination test (*see* below).

The main reason for testing is that immature compost added to soil can cause a temporary reduction in the availability of nitrogen and oxygen and

Putting compost to good use.

Pallet bin contents being sieved (sifted) using a coarse mesh.

Slightly more lumpy compost taken from an Aerobin. The bin has a central aeration system, so the material is not turned after being added.

Finished compost ready for harvesting in a Hotbin. This is often slightly moister and finer in structure than the compost from a pallet bin.

More finished compost from a Hotbin at the Stokes Wood demonstration site, used for food waste from the café. The eggshells that are still visible will be crushed and put back into the bin.

create root-inhibiting organic acids. If it has been produced using a cold-composting system it can also add weed seeds, pests and plant pathogens to the picture. Because of this, during the growing season immature compost is best used as a surface mulch. It may, however, be dug into garden beds during the autumn and winter. Alternatively, it can be stored in a covered heap or bin until it is fully mature.

Sieving or Sifting the Compost

Most home compost is used as a mulch and will not need sieving, although on community sites a coarse sieve may be needed to extract any uncomposted sticks and deal with the larger lumps. If the compost is to be used for sowing seeds or potting up seedlings, for lawn dressing or to top up pots, sieving or sifting will be beneficial. The main issue with this is that most sieves get clogged up quickly if the compost is wet or even moist. This can be avoided by using only matured compost that has dried off during the curing process. If planning to use compost fresh from a working bin it might be advisable to allow it to dry a little before sieving.

A basic hand sieve in plastic or metal will be adequate for small amounts of home-produced compost, but if larger quantities are being made – for

Compost maturity tests

Where a community composting scheme is planning to sell its compost, formal testing and certification may be required. This can be undertaken by approved third-party organisations. Most home and community composters rely on visual inspection, feel and smell to confirm that their compost is ready for use, but the three-day bag test is nonetheless recommended for all batches. A sample of the compost is sealed in a plastic bag and put aside for three days. If it still smells pleasant after the bag is reopened, the composting process has finished.

A simple germination (or radish) test can also be used. This is advisable where any of the compost feedstock has been imported from outside the home site or where horse or farmyard manure has been used as an activator. Radish seeds are sown in a sample of the compost and left to germinate. If more than three-quarters of the seedlings seem to be healthy and free from deformity, the compost has passed the test. Radish seeds tend to be used because they generally germinate relatively quickly, but the test may also be carried out with French or broad beans, peas and tomatoes seeds.

Hand-held sieves are useful for small amounts of compost.

A simple home-made sieve.

Using a compost sieve. Designed for ease of storage, this type of sieve is used with small quantities of compost.

A home-made coarse sieve can be mounted on legs to give a comfortable working height and directly fill a bag or wheelbarrow. It is seen alongside two small fine sieves.

example, potting compost on an allotment – a little assistance may be required. It is not too difficult to make simple sieves of weldmesh fixed to the bottom of a square wooden frame, using a wider mesh to remove larger lumps and a finer one for sifting compost for potting. These sieves also work best with dry compost.

Sieves can also be made to be fitted on a wheelbarrow, with a hopper that will take up to about eight spadefuls of soil. For really large quantities it may be worth considering a rotary sieve, known as a trommel, turned either manually or by a motor. There are commercial models available for purchase, but a home-made version could also be made by following a plan downloaded from the internet.

A home-made rotating cylindrical sieve (trommel). There are many ideas online for home-made rotary sieves.

Free-standing sieve where the compost is thrown against the mesh and only the finer material passes through.

A rotary soil sieve being used to produce a finer compost.

Trommel rotary sieve with motor.

Uses of Compost

Compost consists of organic matter laced with the microbes that helped make it. Adding compost to soil will not only improve the biological properties of the soil but also help provide a good physical structure and some of the necessary chemical nutrients. It will improve the moisture retention of sandy soils and, over time, drainage and aeration in clay soils. As the increased organic material in the compost encourages earthworms and other microbes, it is understandable that the most common use of home-produced compost is as a surface mulch.

No-Dig and Minimum-Dig Gardening

It is now generally accepted that the less soil is dug, disturbing the structure and underground microbial activity, the better. Compost is ideal for use in no-dig, or minimum-dig, gardening, where it is spread on the ground surface as a mulch about 3–15cm (1.5–6in) deep and left for the worms to take it down into the soil. Adopting no-dig can make future gardening easier and increase the productivity of the plot. The initial no-dig plot should be relatively small so that it can be worked without standing on it, to prevent compacting the soil.

Preparation for a new bed is relatively simple. The ground is cleared of weeds and a layer of cardboard put down to deprive any remaining weeds of light. The cardboard is then covered with a 15cm (6in) layer of compost. Once they have been mulched with compost, the beds can be left to settle for a few days before being planted up. If seeds are to be sown in it, the bed should be topped up with a layer of sieved compost.

The compost is often spread in this way in the spring, but it can be done at any time of year. It should be topped up annually for the next four years by adding 3 to 5cm (1.5 to 2in) of compost to replace the material that has been carried down into the soil by the worms. After that time, it will be necessary to add more compost only when the soil becomes visible through the compost that has already been spread.

Home-produced compost can be used in a minimum-dig seedbed by spreading it at a rate of five bucketfuls per square metre and forking it into the top 5cm (2in) of soil.

Finished and sieved compost ready for use.

Using compost on cardboard to reduce weed growth.

Compost can be used in both the flower garden and the vegetable garden.

When mulching an existing flower border, the compost should be applied around the plants but not touching them.

Mulch

As well as mature compost, unfinished (non-matured) compost can also be used, avoiding the need to store it through the maturation stage. If it is spread as a mulch over the flower or vegetable bed in the autumn, the worms will take it down into the soil, where it will replenish much-needed nutrients and help reduce soil erosion. A layer of 5cm (2in) is recommended, leaving a gap around any soft-stemmed plants. Adding mulch after it has rained will help the moisture to be retained in the soil.

There are a few variations to the basic mulch techniques that can be used:

- **In the flower bed**: the compost can be applied as a thin mulch and left on the surface around but not touching the plants, where digging it in would damage roots or bulbs. A 10cm (4in) layer of compost can also be dug into the soil prior to planting.
- **In the vegetable plot**: as an alternative to a surface mulch, the compost can be spread and then dug into the soil in the autumn. This will supply nutrients and humus to the root zone of the plants before planting in the spring or early summer. On sandy soils, compost mulch can be spread over the surface to form a 2–3cm (1–1.5in) layer and then dug into the soil to just over half the length of the blade of a digging spade. On clay soils, the quantity can be doubled. However, unmatured compost, in which the decomposition process is not completed, should not be dug into the soil immediately before planting.

This may cause stress to the plants, resulting in a yellowing of the leaves and stalled growth. The amount of compost to use in the vegetable plot will vary, depending on how much is available and the use of that area of the garden. The general recommendation is a wheelbarrow load spread over 5 square metres before planting. Over-wintering brassicas will benefit from a summer mulch. Fruit grown in the vegetable garden can be mulched every four or five years.

- **As a mulch around established trees**: a 5–10cm (2–4in) layer of compost applied twice a year can provide nutrients and help with water retention in a soil that otherwise may be neglected and depleted. A gap should be left around the trunks of trees.

A pumpkin patch that has been treated with a mulch and aerated compost tea.

Direct Sowing

An open compost bin or heap can be used to grow courgettes, marrows and squashes by direct sowing, allowing more food to be produced in a relatively small garden without making a permanent vegetable plot. The seeds may be sown directly on the bin or heap and left to germinate and grow, or they may be germinated elsewhere and transplanted into the bin or heap as seedlings. It is also quite likely that 'volunteer' plants may grow from tomato or pumpkin seeds on the material being composted. Once they have germinated, they can be left in the compost or transplanted to another location. If they are left growing in the bin, the compost cannot be harvested until the autumn but that is no hardship compared with the benefits.

Raised Beds and 'Square-Foot' Gardening

When preparing a raised bed, matured compost can be used as a mulch or mixed with various materials such as clay, sand and even aged sawdust. The compost should not exceed more than 30 per cent of the total mix. Lasagne composting (*see* Chapter 2) can be used to fill a raised bed. The bed can be filled as compost is produced over the season before use is required.

This intensive gardening in deep raised beds divided into one-foot squares uses compost as a key part of the soil mix, and as a soil amendment during use of the bed. Include a handful of compost each time anything

is added to the bed, working it into the soil top layers. New seeds can be sown in the newly enriched soil.

Top Dressing for Lawns

Top dressing a lawn with compost can improve the soil structure and provide some nutrients. It will also improve drainage by adding organic matter to the lawn and can also be used to fill holes and depressions.

A top dressing of 1–2cm (half an inch) of compost is often applied to the lawn in the autumn, but it can also be used in the spring to start the season. It should be done early, though, when there will be less footfall, reducing the likelihood of compost being carried indoors. Sweeping it into the grass with a broom will also help reduce the risk of this occurring.

The value of more frequent but lighter applications of compost as a top dressing is now being recognised. If adopting this routine of treatment, the first layer is best applied early in spring, and it can then be repeated every month in places where the lawn is used regularly. It is best to sieve or break up the compost, as smaller particles will more easily drop between the blades of grass and become incorporated into the soil. It is best applied dry.

Before dressing the lawn, the grass should be mowed to 2.5cm (an inch) tall and dead grass, leaves and other lawn debris raked up and collected.

If the compost heap or bin has taken about as much grass as it can handle and sending grass cuttings to the council composting site is too costly as an

Pumpkins will grow readily on the compost heap.

Top dressing and sweeping compost into a lawn.

option, it may be left on the lawn. The lawn may need more frequent mowing than it does when the grass is taken away and should be mown only when the grass is dry. Apparently, grass clippings can provide about a third of the nutrients that a lawn needs for healthy growth so there will be a saving on the cost of lawn fertiliser too.

Indoor and Patio Plants

Compost can be used to top up pots containing indoor plants and patio plants. The usual approach is to add about 1cm (half an inch) of compost to the top of the pot. To refresh a pot containing an established plant, a layer of the old compost can be removed and replaced with fresh material. When repotting to a larger pot, the compost can be added to the bottom of the new pot.

Home-Made Seed and Potting Compost

When it is fully matured and has been sieved or screened, home compost can be used to make peat-free seed and potting mixes. This is done by heat-treating it in an oven (160°C for an hour) or microwaving in a bag for 2 to 2.5 minutes on full power (650-watt oven).

In addition to providing nutrients, the compost should be nicely free-draining. This will prevent water-logging, which causes seeds and seedlings to rot, but at the same time retain sufficient moisture for the plant to grow. It will need to be capable of containing air spaces so that soil microbes and the roots have oxygen, while being of an even consistency and free from lumps. This favours a light or fine textured mix, but it must be sufficiently firm to retain and support the

Topping up indoor flowerpots.

Table 12.1 Home-made seed compost mixes

Ingredients	Mix
Leaf mould and loam	1 leaf mould:1 loam
Leaf mould, compost and/or loam	1 leaf mould:1 compost:1 loam
Leaf mould (or compost), loam and sharp sand	1 leaf mould:2 loam:1 sand
Leaf mould and worm compost	3 leaf mould:1 worm compost
Compost, loam and sand	1 compost:2 loam:1 sharp sand

Table 12.2 Simple potting mixes

Ingredients	Mix
Leaf mould and loam	1 leaf mould:1 loam
Leaf mould and worm compost	3 leaf mould:1 worm compost
Leaf mould, compost and loam	1 leaf mould:1 compost:1 loam
Leaf mould, compost, loam and sharp sand	1 leaf mould:1 loam:1 compost:1 sand
Leaf mould, loam and mature manure	1 leaf mould:3 loam:1 manure
Compost, loam and sand	1 compost:1 topsoil:1 sharp sand

seedling as it grows to a size suitable for potting on. It should also retain its volume in the pot and be free from pests and disease.

A simple seed compost can consist of 1 part compost to 3 parts compost or soil, but there are other alternatives (see left), most of which involve the use of leaf mould, which is easy to make (see Chapter 5).

Plants that already have roots require more nutritious compost, so a simple potting mixture for transplanting plants should be made up of 1 part compost to 2 parts soil or loam.

Other Uses

Compost can also be used to make compost teas. For information on this, together with methods for making other plant feeds, see Chapter 13.

Compost Use by Professional Gardeners

Compost is also used in various ways on a larger scale by professional, estate or park gardeners. When planting trees and shrubs, it is the ideal material to use as backfill. It offers the necessary support when filling gaps round the rootball, retains moisture and adds nutrients. It can be used on its own or mixed with some of the soil removed when digging the hole for the tree or shrub. Nursery beds can be improved by mixing home-produced compost with soil to create a growing medium with good water retention properties and organic content.

CHAPTER 13

COMPOST TEAS AND LIQUID FEEDS

Traditionally, animal manure soaks have been used as liquid feeds, as has the liquid produced when perennial weeds are drowned to convert them to a form that can be added to a cold-composting bin. Compost (with or without aeration) can also be used to make teas and extracts, which can serve as liquid feeds.

Plant-Derived Liquid Feeds

Drowned Mixed Perennial Plants

Drowning is an effective way of treating the more common native perennial weeds that would survive cool composting, but it is not effective when dealing with perennial bog plants. It has an advantage over drying (desiccation) in that it produces a compost activator that can be added to the compost bin or used as a liquid plant food.

To make the liquid feed, the perennial weeds are put in a suitable container, covered with water and weighed down with a brick or stone. The container is then covered to exclude light, and the contents are left to decompose. Depending on the type of plant material, this may take any time between a month and a year. In the case of couch grass, a year or longer might be required to kill all the roots. When all the plant material

has broken down, the liquid can be poured off carefully and sieved for use as a liquid feed. The remaining sludgy contents can be added to the compost bin.

Green Leaves and Shoots

Drowning perennial weeds will take months or even as long as a year, depending on the type of plant. In

Containers for making liquid feeds and for drowning perennial weeds.

contrast, a nutritious liquid feed (or 'plant tea') may be produced in just 48 hours to four weeks by soaking the leaves and green shoots of young plants. There are several different types of plant that can be used to produce liquid feeds in this way, and in most cases several cuts of the plant may be taken in a single season. If the plant material is soaked in rainwater or other unchlorinated water, the resulting feed will provide a natural source of nutrients and a kinder alternative to the chemical fertilisers that may harm insects, wildlife, plants and the soil. Ideally, rainwater collected from the roofs of sheds or greenhouses is best. If rainwater is not available and tap water has to be used, it should be left standing in the container for at least two days. After this, the pH should be checked, and a little spirit vinegar added if it needs acidifying to bring it to a more neutral level.

When making liquid feeds the young, green parts of the plant are normally used, carefully avoiding the roots of perennial plants and seeds, which may survive the process. Chopping and tearing the greenery into small pieces will speed up the decomposition.

During the fermentation period, dissolved oxygen will reach low levels, encouraging anaerobic microbial growth, but this will not be the case throughout the whole soaking period. Towards the end of the soak some aerobic organisms will become active as oxygen returns to the liquid. The effectiveness of the process can be influenced by the temperature. Biological decomposition will occur best at temperatures favourable to the microorganisms involved – within the range of 12°C to 25°C.

Using the Liquid Feeds

Once finished, the liquid feeds are best diluted, again using unchlorinated water such as rainwater. Naturally, there will be variations between the 'tea' produced by different plants and different gardeners will suggest different dilutions. In general, when diluting the solution resulting from drowning perennial weeds, it should be approximately 5–10 parts rainwater to 1 part weed water. As a guide, the watered-down solution should look like weak tea, but the colours will vary according to the type and amounts of plant material that have been soaked.

Filtered plant teas can be applied either by watering the soil or as a foliar spray.

Equipment

The traditional method of making plant liquid feeds involved soaking young growth weighed down in the water with a stone or other weight. The liquid was carefully tipped off and filtered through a sack, pillow-case, or old pair of tights so that it could be applied using a watering can fitted with a rose or sprayed. If the sludge is not filtered, it will block the rose of the watering can or spray when being applied. A variation that avoids the need to filter the finished liquid involves soaking the material in a sack, a pair of tights, nylon stocking, sock, or another porous bag-like material to hold the compost, or a commercially available mesh compost tea bag (sometimes sold as a compost sock) suspended from a piece of wood across the top of the vessel. An alternative is to tie the bag with a string, the end of which is kept outside the water butt. If using this method, a stone can be put in the bottom of the bag to keep it submerged. The liquid should be stirred frequently. Ideally the container would have a lid, as the product may have an unpleasant odour.

As gardens have become smaller, with less plant material available to utilise as a soak, and little space to hide an extra water butt, several smaller-capacity systems have come on the market. These include the Hozelock Biomix, which enables the householder to make 19 litres of concentrated feed easily and without mess. It is not cheap, but it is easy to use and clean. It comes complete with a lid with a handle that allows the greens to be agitated in the water without opening

After soaking weeds in a dustbin to drown them, the resulting liquid can be used as a feed.

The Hozelock plant food maker has a handle on the lid and paddles for aerating the water.

Young growth for making comfrey tea liquid feed. The leaves should be torn or cut before soaking and the tea can also be used as an activator.

the container. This means that the smell associated with bucket methods of making tea can be prevented. It also has an integral strainer and tap so that the finished tea can be drained off.

Popular Types of Plant Teas and Liquid Feeds

Comfrey Tea

Comfrey is the most popular of the plant teas and is a good source of potassium and nitrogen. Comfrey is a fast-growing and fast-spreading perennial that grows wild on many allotment sites. If it is not found growing wild, it can be introduced by buying root cuttings of the Bocking 14 variety, which is sterile and will not spread by seed.

The most common method of making comfrey tea involves harvesting young leaves about 5cm (2in) above soil level, cutting or tearing them and submerging them in a lidded barrel or tub of rainwater. Approximately 1kg of leaves can be added to every 15 litres of water. The leaves should be pressed down into the container by a brick or broken paving slab and soaked for three to five weeks. This will produce a liquid with a very unpleasant smell, so it is not recommended for use in a greenhouse or polytunnel.

Any lidded container, such as a bucket or water butt, can be used, depending on the volume being made. If the container has a tap or a hole in the bottom the fertiliser can be run off or allowed to drip into a catch-pot. Otherwise, the liquid can be dipped out from the top with a watering can. An old bokashi bin makes an excellent comfrey tea maker for the smaller garden as the filter tray prevents the leaves from blocking the drain tap and the airtight lid contains the smell. The tea is used diluted in a ratio of 1 part tea to 3 parts water for established plants, either watering into the soil or as a foliar spray. For younger, more tender plants, such as tomatoes, it should be diluted 1 part tea to 10 parts water and added to the soil. A similar technique can be used to make nettle tea.

Concentrated comfrey tea is produced in a different way and has the advantage of not smelling as much as the dilute version. It can be made using a drainage pipe fitted with an end cap through which a single drainage

Comfrey soaking. The bucket would normally be lidded to contain the smell.

Soaking comfrey in a Hozelock plant food maker.

hole has been drilled. The comfrey leaves are compressed in the pipe by squashing down with a plastic bottle filled with sand or water, or a sparkling wine bottle, which is heavier and more fun to empty before use in the tube. Larger quantities can be made by packing comfrey leaves into a water butt fitted with a tap, compressing the comfrey to get the maximum amount in and keeping it compressed during fermentation with a weighted slab. A small volume of water or urine and water can be added initially to speed up the process.

Dandelion Tea

The dandelion is a weed that can be turned into a liquid plant feed, with the remaining sludge being composted. The weeds and roots are submerged in rainwater in a 5-gallon lidded bucket, either loose in the water or in a porous sack, and the liquid is stirred at least once a week. It will smell, hence the lid. After two to four weeks, it is stirred for a final time, filtered and then used as a soil fertiliser. The liquid should be diluted 1 part weed tea to 10 parts water, and may be used on soil around plants or as a foliar spray, but not on vegetables that are soon to be harvested. The sludge can be added to the compost bin.

Grass Clippings Liquid Feed

Grass clippings are readily available in most gardens and are frequently home composted or left on the lawn to be absorbed. They can also be soaked to make a liquid fertilizer with a high potash content.

The conventional lidded-bucket soaking method can be used, with a ratio of 10 to 1 water to grass

Comfrey tea concentrate. The comfrey leaves are compressed in the drainpipe by an empty sparkling wine or sand-filled plastic bottle.

clippings by weight. A satisfactory mix may also be obtained by relying on a less accurate visual assessment, where the bucket is two-thirds filled with fresh grass clippings and then topped up with water. A compost tea sock or old pair of tights can be used to contain the grass. The mixture is left to soak for three to five days, then the liquid is squeezed out through the sock or tights and used within 24 hours.

Horsetail Liquid Feed

Horsetail (*Equisetum arvense*) is a relatively common invasive weed that deserves a special mention. It has a thick, silica-rich outer layer and small, needle-like leaves. It can be drowned, as with other perennial weeds. The fermentation time necessary to kill it can range from 10 days to three weeks, depending on the ambient temperature. When it has finished bubbling, the liquid can be strained and used. It is said to have fungicidal properties, so when used to coat the leaves of plants it can protect against blackspot, mildew and mint rust.

Horsetail is an invasive perennial weed, but thorough soaking will result in a liquid plant feed and a sludge that can be added to the compost bin.

Horsetail collected ready to soak. It will be submerged using a brick.

Seaweed Liquid Feed

Seaweed contains plant nutrients, including potassium (up to 12%) but it is low in nitrogen and phosphate. It can contain around 60 trace elements, growth hormones and other nutrients, and is particularly rich in iodine and calcium. Spraying seaweed tea on plants is said to increase their resistance to insect infestation.

The collection of seaweed is regulated by laws designed to protect the marine environment. In the UK, the Crown Estate licenses sustainable, commercial harvesting of seaweed from areas of foreshore and seabed that are not privately owned. Collection in small qualities for personal use does not require a licence, but the permission of the landowner should be sought.

The seaweed should be rinsed to remove excess salt and then submerged in a bucket of water for about eight weeks in the dark. The resulting liquid should be diluted 1:2 before use.

Banana Peel Liquid Feed

Banana peel is said to make a good liquid feed because of its relatively high potassium content. Banana skins are readily available in many primary schools and are relatively clean, so make a good source of liquid feed for a school garden club. The simplest method is to put the banana peel in a jar or bucket, cover with water and soak for two to seven days, although it can be left for longer. Banana peel tea can also be made in a Hozelock Biomix, with 1kg banana peel, collected from friends and family and other allotment plot-holders, and 10 litres of water.

Making banana skin liquid feed is a good project for primary schools. With the plant food maker, 1kg of banana peel should be soaked in 10 litres of water.

Banana peel tea can be stirred and aerated without opening the lid. Stirring should be repeated at least daily for three weeks.

Banana tea after two weeks. The unfiltered solution is cloudy, and pieces of banana peel are still visible.

Finished and bottled banana tea from the plant food maker. It is filtered within the equipment as it empties.

Making Compost Tea

The decomposed organic matter present in compost improves soil quality and provides nutrients for the plants. However, the billions of bacteria, fungi, protozoa, nematodes and other microorganisms that form the living components of compost are often forgotten once they have completed their role in making the compost.

Compost tea increases the benefits of normal composting by boosting the microbes in the soil and acts as a liquid fertiliser supplying soluble nutrients that can be used by plants. It can be used either as a foliar spray and it can be applied to soil. It cannot be over-applied and can be used at any time of year. It is recommended for use on plants every 14–30 days during the growing season. However, it can be applied as often as once a week to help control disease or when soil quality is poor.

Compost tea should not be confused with compost leachate, which is the liquid that has percolated through and drained from the feedstock in the compost bin or wormery. Leachate consists of extracted, dissolved or suspended materials, including organisms, from a mix of immature and mature compost collected as the water passes through the heap.

Selecting the Compost

The key to making good compost tea is the quality of the initial compost. The best home-made compost is the mature product from a hot heap as this will tend to have a good supply of beneficial microbes and higher fungal counts than that from a cold compost heap. If possible, it is worth checking for the presence of bacteria, fungi and protozoa using a microscope. The added benefit of hot composting is that it also kills potential pathogens. Where the fungal count is known to be low it can be increased in any compost by the addition of fish hydrolysate a couple of weeks before brewing. Another way of increasing the fungal count in the compost before use in making tea is to mix it with a small handful of coarse oatmeal (UK) or steel cut oats (USA) for at least two weeks before brewing.

As an alternative to using home compost, specially formulated compost for use in making compost tea can be purchased from brewing equipment suppliers. This has been formulated to provide a balanced compost that is rich in bacteria, fungi and protozoa.

The water used to make all the teas should be free from chlorine. Rainwater is ideal but if chlorinated water must be used it should be stood overnight before starting the tea. The pH of the water should be near to neutral, within the range 6.5–7.5. The pH of the finished tea should be 6.8–7.2. There are ways of adjusting it, if necessary.

Compost tea can be either non-aerated or aerated. Each type has its own merits.

Non-Aerated Compost Tea (NCT)

NCT is made by simply soaking sweet-smelling mature aerobic compost in water. Soaking and stirring removes microbes as well as soluble nutrients from the compost so that the finished tea will contain the range of enzymes, hormones, microbes, nutrients and plant growth compounds found in the original compost. The tea will reach low oxygen levels but with regular stirring they should not fall below 5.5ppm. The full food web may be present if oxygen levels do not drop below this level.

On the allotment or in the garden this procedure is convenient, requiring little time and effort as the compost is simply soaked and periodically stirred by hand.

If it is not stirred frequently, NCT may contain non-beneficial anaerobes because the air surface of the container cannot provide enough oxygen for microbes in the lower portions of the container to respire aerobically. The likelihood of anaerobic conditions occurring increases if the compost used is immature. One of the reasons that non-aerated compost teas do not normally have additional food sources added to the brew is that this will also increase the likelihood of anaerobic conditions. Tea in which anaerobic conditions have been allowed to develop will be less effective as a foliar feed.

Compost tea was traditionally made by suspending a bag of some kind – a sack, cheesecloth bag, pillowcase or old pair of tights – containing compost in a barrel or bucket of water for seven to 14 days. The bag is suspended by string from a rod across the top of the bucket or from a skirt hanger so that the compost is completely submerged (a stone can be added to the bag as a weight). Although some methods suggest holding the sack on the bottom of the bucket using a stone, the sack should preferably be held off the container base to aid circulation. The microbes will be filtered through the material to give a liquid feed that can be applied with a watering can or a sprayer.

Compost extract is a variation on this theme in which the compost is not allowed time to 'brew'. It can be made in minutes by shaking bagged compost vigorously in a bucket of rainwater or running water at pressure through compost. It is recommended to repeat the process after 10–15 minutes. Making compost extract requires a larger volume of compost than making aerated teas. It can be used as a soil drench, a root dip during transplanting or as an activator added to compost heaps.

Compost extract can be created by agitating a bag of compost at about 15-minute intervals.

The technique has been modified slightly over the years, using different water containers – for example, buckets or water butts – and filtering the liquid before use, rather than soaking in a bag. Under this 'free compost' variation, which makes it easier to aerate the mix and mechanically remove organisms by stirring, the compost is left loose in the water and filtered at the end of the process through muslin or an old pair of tights to avoid it blocking the watering can rose when it is being

Simple basic non-aerated compost tea, three- to four-day brew

1. A bucket is filled one-third full of mature compost and rainwater added to just below the top. If using chlorinated tap water, the bucket should be filled at least the night before.
2. The mix is left to soak for between three days and several weeks. The longer the period and more frequent the stirring to aerate the mix, the more organisms will be extracted from the compost. The longer the periods between stirring, the more likely that the resultant feed will contain a high proportion of anaerobes.
3. After the soaking period, the liquid is strained through an old pair of tights, cheesecloth or other porous fabric into a second bucket.
4. The filtered liquid is diluted with rainwater until it is the colour of weak tea, or in a 10:1 ratio of water: tea, and used immediately.

applied. A short length of plastic downpipe with the leg of a pair of tights over one end works well as a reusable filter.

Finished worm compost is an excellent compost for making compost tea. It can be used on its own or 50:50 with conventional compost, ideally prepared in a hot-composting system dealing with predominately green waste.

Actively Aerated Compost Tea (ACT or AACT)

Aerated compost tea (ACT) offers certain advantages over tea made without aeration: it contains more active microorganisms, due to the aeration and the presence of a microbial food source such as molasses, kelp or rock dust. It will contain bacteria, fungi, protozoa and nematodes, which all play a role in soil health and, it is said, promote growth and resistance to disease. The use of ACT as a foliar spray is more controversial.

Aerator and container for making aerated compost tea.

Compost tea made in a compost 'teabag', before aeration.

Aeration in progress.

Aerated tea in a bucket

1. Half-fill a 5-gallon bucket with compost, breaking up any lumps, or add the same quantity of compost to a compost teabag and suspend in the bucket. Fill with rainwater to within 3 or 4 inches of the top.
2. About an ounce of black treacle (molasses) or another food source can be added to the compost or stirred into the water.
3. If a compost tea aerator of the correct size is used, the bubbles will agitate the whole solution. If an aquarium aerator is used, the solution may also need to be stirred regularly throughout the 2- to 3-day brewing process.
4. At the end of the aeration period, the pump is turned off. If the compost was loose in the water, the brew will need to be left to settle for about 30 minutes before being carefully poured off and filtered without disturbing the sludge, which can be added to the compost bin. If a bag was used to contain the compost it can be removed, and the remains of the compost added directly to a compost bin.
5. As an alternative to black treacle, white sugar (1 tablespoon per gallon) can be mixed with the compost. An additional source of nutrients such as nettle or comfrey tea or liquid seaweed can also be added to the mix.

Nutrients are said to be absorbed through the leaves and the beneficial microbes it contains may influence plant pathogens present.

Worm castings make excellent ACT as the compost is high in beneficial microorganisms and a good

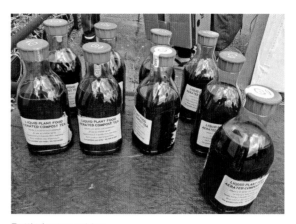

Bottled compost tea.

source of humic acid. If worm castings are not available, a mature aerobic hot compost will suffice. Constant aeration during the brewing process, providing at least 6ppm of dissolved oxygen and enough bubbles to agitate the liquid, create the conditions for a 24- to 36-hour aerobic brewing period.

The tea-making process is usually facilitated by the addition of nutrients – for example, black molasses/treacle or kelp, or liquid plant extract such as nettle soup, comfrey tea or even dandelion wine – to the brew to assist the microbe growth. They can also be added to the finished tea immediately before application. These additives may be purchased premixed as 'compost tea catalysts'.

The simplest and cheapest method of making ACT is in a bucket aerated by aquarium bubblers. There are many variations suitable for use by home composters using a 20-litre or 5-gallon bucket aerated by two aquarium aerator stones or bubblers powered by a aquarium pump of a good size. Specialist compost tea bubblers, which give a more even air distribution, are also available commercially.

Compost Bin Leachate

All compost bins and heaps produce leachate. This is the liquid that seeps from the decomposing organic material and can be a significant pollutant when composting is undertaken on a commercial scale. The chemical and physical nature of the compost leachate is important as the liquid can migrate into, and pollute, underlying soils and groundwater, while the run-off can contaminate ditches, ponds and streams. This is not normally a problem with domestic compost bins as relatively little leachate is produced and the liquid will be absorbed by the soil. With most home open-bottom composting systems, the leachate drains away into the soil but there are modern compost bins with bases that allow leachate to be collected. Leachate can also be collected from tumbler bins by installing a drip tray, or other form of containment, beneath the drum. The tray may be fitted with a drainage tube so that the leachate can be collected in a bucket. Drip trays should be emptied regularly so that they do not overflow. Leachate can be added to the compost bin both to increase the moisture content in dry weather and as an activator.

Rain falling on to an uncovered bin or heap can add to the leachate run-off and increase the risk of contamination of groundwater or any water courses adjacent to the composting area. While the composting material needs to stay moist to decompose properly, it should not be allowed to become waterlogged or produce significant amounts of run-off. Covering the heap with a tarpaulin or fitting a lid on the bin will reduce this risk. Hot-composting systems using a New Zealand bin or a modern composter such as the Hotbin tend to produce less leachate as a considerable volume of the water evaporates. The amount of leachate produced will increase when food waste with a high moisture content is being composted.

If the compost bin or heap is mounted directly on the soil, moving it every two or three years allows the area fertilised by the leachate to be utilised for growing. Alternatively, the bin could be standing on a waterproof membrane, which is drained into a bucket set into the ground. If a permanent composting area is being used, the heaps or bins can be stood on a concrete bed or slabs sloping to a gutter, which drains into a bucket set into the ground to collect the leachate. It is advisable to use a lidded bucket or have a wooden cover over it to reduce the ingress of rainwater, which would dilute the leachate.

There is a view that leachate should not be used, as food scraps and garden waste all carry bacteria, fungi and parasites, and it may also have been contaminated during decomposition by the faeces of rats, birds, and so on. Leachate from home composting is more likely to contain pathogens if:

- contaminated food waste has been added to the bin; or
- rats, birds or other creatures have gained access; or
- manure has been used, particularly in a cold-composting system.

The types and potential pathogenicity of the microorganisms present in the compost and leachate will vary depending on the materials being composted. Manure and waste meat, for example, are high-risk source ingredients. Normally, the pathogens will be destroyed by competition from other materials in the bin and by the heat during hot composting. Faecal bacteria such as *E. coli* in compost may also contaminate vegetables that are grown in it. This could pose a health risk to humans if the vegetables are eaten without adequate washing and cooking.

Making compost without the addition of manure reduces the risk of contamination by faecal coliforms but there may still be some plant organisms present that are capable of causing human disease. The risks from leachate contamination can also be reduced by using potable water to soak and maintain the moisture level during the composting process. However, many will prefer to use rainwater collected in covered water butts from the roofs of outbuildings and sheds. Some will use pond or stream water, but in this case the area around the pond or stream should be checked to ensure that it is not being contaminated by seepage from stored manure, manure applied to adjacent land or farm livestock.

In addition to containing microorganisms, the leachate will contain dissolved chemicals and larger organic and suspended inorganic particulates such as colloids. The leachate will also contain nutrients beneficial to plants, such as nitrogen and potassium, fulvic acid and humic acid. The dissolved and particulate organic matter gives the leachate its characteristic yellow to dark brown colour. During the initial decomposition, the leachate contains oxidised functional groups. In the later stages, as the compost matures and the plant lignin in the material decomposes, more phenolic groups are present. The highest concentrations of organic matter, nutrients and contaminants are found in the initial leachate and those concentrations will decrease as the material is diluted by rainwater, if it is permitted to run through the compost.

If it is fresh, odour-free and light brown in colour, the leachate may be spread on the plot or garden and used as a liquid fertiliser around plants. The normal dilution rate is 1:10 leachate to water but for more sensitive plants a ratio of 1:20 is recommended.

Manure Teas

There are a number of recipes for manure teas. The simplest method is to soak a spade full of manure in a bucket of rainwater, to give a dilution of about one-third manure to two-thirds water, for between three days and a week, stirring frequently. After the last stirring, the contents should be allowed to settle for an hour before the liquid is carefully poured off or filtered. Alternatively, the manure can be soaked in a commercially available compost teabag, an old pair of tights, pillowcase or sack and suspended in a bucket of rainwater for about two weeks. As with other teas, the resulting liquid feed should be diluted before use – in a ratio of about 250ml tea to 4.5 litres of rainwater – until it is the colour of weak tea.

While manure was used to make liquid feed by many gardeners in the past, it has recently fallen from favour due to the potential for infection. These concerns are justified as faecal bacteria such as salmonella, listeria and *E. coli* 0157 have been associated with contamination of vegetables. Human parasites such as *Cryptosporidium parvum* and *Giardia lamblia* may also be present. The risks can be reduced by allowing the manure to mature for a year before using it. Plants may also be left for 120 days before harvesting if the edible part is in contact with treated soil or has been sprayed with manure tea. Good hygiene procedures should always be followed, including thoroughly washing the hands after handling the manure or tea and after harvesting the produce. To be honest, it is difficult to justify the continued use of manure teas if there is an alternative available.

ACKNOWLEDGEMENTS

Thanks must go to those staff at Garden Organic and the Leicestershire Country Council Master Composter programme who have offered help, advice and encouragement over the years, the representatives of the National Allotments Society and the committee at Stokes Wood Allotments. I would also like to acknowledge the help, enthusiasm and knowledge of National Trust gardeners throughout the UK.

I am indebted to the following composters for permission to use their photographs:

Chapter 2: P. Hutchings p.23 (bottom right, p.27 (middle right); Asmita Kabra p.31
Chapter 4: Justin McNeil p.67 (top left)
Chapter 6: Biolan Oy p.82 (top right and bottom right), p.90 (bottom). Chris Poolman p.92
Chapter 7: Holly Kurzha p.97 (top right); Georgina Armour-Langham p.109 (top right, bottom left)
Chapter 8: Russell Chambers p.116; Lorna Abrahams p.115 (top left)
Chapter 10: Wiggy Wigglers p.137 (top right); Ron Heath p.139 (top left)
Chapter 12: Wendy Bull p.158 (right); Donal O'Leary p.157 (top left); Peter Brook p.157 (top right); David Hammon p.157 (bottom right); Marc Lamothe p.160 (left)

Thanks are also due to Barbara Weston for her help and patience as composting took over my life, and compost bins and equipment for stands and training sessions filled the garage.

As my interest in composting developed over the years, I have collect a small library of books on the subject. The following relatively recent books have been a major source of information and are recommended further reading:

How to Make and Use Compost by Nicky Scott (2009). Green Books

The Garden Organic Book of Compost (2011), New Holland Publishers (UK) Ltd

Bokashi Composting by Adam Footer (2014), New Society Publishers. This was a very helpful source on this specialized subject

I have also made use of a number of earlier books to provide information on traditional techniques and topics, such as the use of bigger bins in large gardens and anaerobic 'composting':

Compost Gardening by W. E. Shewell-Cooper (1974), David & Charles

The Rodale Book of Composting by Grace Gershuny & Deborah L. Martin (eds) (1992). Rodale Press

The Rodale Guide to Composting (1979) by Jerry Minnich, Marjorie Hunt et al.

US fact sheets and guidance

Fact sheets and other publications available on the internet also provide a source of useful information, particularly:

Compost Happens Tutorial, Florida's Online Composting Centre (2011). University of Florida

Cornell Waste Management Fact Sheets, Cornell University, Ithaca, NY

The Rapid Composting Method by Robert D Raabe (1992). University of California

On-Farm Composting Handbook. Robert Rynk (ed.), Northeast Regional Agricultural Engineering Service. Cornell University, Ithaca, NY

Community composting

The Community Composting Guide by Community Composting Network: Nicky Scott, Nick McAllister et al. Resource Publishing Ltd. The CCN has been incorporated into the Social Farms and Garden organisation.

Community-Scale Composting Systems by James McSweeney (2019). Chelsea Green Publishing

INDEX.

actively aerated compost tea (AACT)
170–171
aerated compost tea (ACT) 170–171
aerobic composting 17
  vs. anaerobic digestion 12, 51
anaerobic digestion or
      fermentation 12, 17
  barrel or bucket 34
  bokashi method 32
  covered heap 34
  oxidation process 31
  in sealed bag or sack 32–34
  submersion composting 35
  using a bin 34–35
aspergillosis 122

biochar 14
Biolan garden composter 82
bokashi fermentation
  in bins 148–150
  bokashi tea or juice 150–151
  fungal mould 151
  pre-compost 152
  soil factory 152–153
  in windrows 146–148

commercial vermiculture 132
compost
  maturity tests 154–156
  by professional gardeners 162
  sieving or sifting 155–157
  uses
    compost teas 162
    direct sowing 160
    home-made seed and
        potting 161–162
    indoor and patio plants 161
    mulch 159
    no-dig, and minimum-dig
        gardening 158
    raised beds and 'square-foot'
        gardening 160
    top dressing for lawns 160–161
compost activators
  coffee grounds 129
  compost or soil 130
  green plants 128
  home-made aerated compost tea
      (ACT) 130–131
  human urine 130
  hydrated lime or dolomite 131
  inoculators 131
  in layered bin or heap 127–128
  manures 128–129
  powdered natural products 130
  seaweed 130

composting
  aerobic home and allotment
      composting 13–14
  anaerobic digestion or
      fermentation 12
    barrel or bucket 34
    bokashi method 32
    covered heap 34
    oxidation process 31
    in sealed bag or sack 32–34
    submersion composting 35
    using a bin 34–35
  bacterial activity and
      temperature 52
  basic requirements of 36
    moisture 42–43
    oxygen and aeration 37–40
    temperature 40–42
  carbon and nitrogen 44
  and climate change 11–13
  community composting
      sites 14–16
  compost bin leachate 171–172
  containers for outdoors
    for cooked food 28–29
    gravity-fed bins 26
    moulded plastic bins 24–25
    sectional plastic bins 25
    for small or hard-landscaped
        gardens 29–30
    tumbler bins 28
    wooden bins 27–28
    wormeries 29
  country-house composting 16
  cycle of 11
  food waste, option for 21
  garden waste, option for 20
  health and safety 18–19
  hierarchy 11
  history of 8–9
  hot composting
    active 107–108
    Berkeley method 108
    vs. cold 59
    curing or maturation
        stage 57–58, 101–102,
        109–110
    disease-causing
        microorganisms 59
    mesophilic phase 55–56,
        99–100
    no-turn methods 108–109
    pre-composting storage
        space 102–103
    psychrophilic
        microorganisms 55, 98–99

  temperature maintenance
      106–107
  thermophilic organisms 56–57,
      100–101
  traditional methods 103–106
  using traditional bins 102
Hügelkultur method 22–23
indoor
  plastic storage boxes 30–31
  shredded paper or cardboard 30
  techniques 31
  terracotta containers 31
larger quantities 93–96
lasagne composting 22
levels of organisms 37
methods and techniques 17–18
microorganisms
  actinomycetes 50
  aerobic bacteria 51
  anaerobic bacteria 51–52
  bacteria 49–50
  fungi 51
  protozoa and rotifers 51
nutrient concentrations, balance
      of 44
pH scale 49
post-hole composting 22
sheet composting 22
stages of 52
traditional compost heap or pile 23
trench composting 22
compost teas 162, 168
  actively aerated compost tea
      (AACT) 170–171
  compost selection 168
  non-aerated compost tea
      (NCT) 169–170
contained wormeries 136–138
containers for outdoor composting
  for cooked food 28–29
  gravity-fed bins 26
  moulded plastic bins 24–25
  sectional plastic bins 25
  for small or hard-landscaped
      gardens 29–30
  tumbler bins 28
  wooden bins 27–28
  wormeries 29

Degradation, Conversion
      and Maturation (DCM)
      Classification 52

effective microorganisms (EM) 145
entry-level composting systems
  adding waste to a bin 69–70

with different materials
    asbestos cement sheet 65–66
    builders' bags 64
    concrete slabs and bricks 64
    metal sheeting and weldmesh 64
    old tyres 64–65
grass boarding 74–75
harvesting the compost 71–72
Hügelkultur mound 76–77
lasagne composting 75
leaf mould, making of 72–73
locate the bin 66
materials
    garden waste 67
    kitchen waste 67–68
    other household waste 68
plastic compost bins
    advantages of 60
    hatch types 61
post-hole composting 75–76
sheet composting 74
trench composting 75
wooden bins 63

garden wormeries
    dug-in worm beds 140
    raised worm beds 139

home vermiculture 133
hot composting
    active 107–108
    Berkeley method 108
    vs. cold 59
    curing or maturation stage 57–58,
        101–102, 109–110
    disease-causing microorganisms 59
    mesophilic phase 55–56,
        99–100
    no-turn methods 108–109
    pre-composting storage
        space 102–103
    psychrophilic microorganisms
        55, 98–99
    temperature maintenance
        106–107
    thermophilic organisms 56–57,
        100–101
    traditional methods 103–106
    using traditional bins 102
Hotrock garden
    composter 82
Hügelkultur method 22–23

indoor composting
    plastic storage boxes 30–31
    shredded paper or cardboard 30
    techniques 31
    terracotta containers 31
indoor wormeries 138
Indore composting method 9

lasagne composting 22, 75
levels of organisms 37

manure teas 172
microorganisms
    actinomycetes 50
    aerobic bacteria 51
    anaerobic bacteria 51–52
    bacteria 49–50
    disease-causing 18–19, 59
    effective 145
    fungi 51
    protozoa and rotifers 51
    psychrophilic 55
microplastic pollution 18
mid- and higher-range compost bins
    for cooked food waste
        Aerobin 89–90
        Biolan 90
        Green Cone food
            digester 85–86
        Green Johanna 86–87
        Hotbin 88–89
        Joraform 91
        Ridan 92
    gravity-fed bins 83
    maturation bins 92
    moulded plastic bins 80–81
    premium plastic bins 82
    sectional compost bins 81
    traditional-style plastic bins 80
    tumbler bins 83–85
    wooden bins
        advantages of 79–80
        factors involved in handling 78
        pressure-treated 78
        slatted sides 79

non-aerated compost tea
    (NCT) 169–170

plant-derived liquid feeds
    banana peel 167
    comfrey tea 165–166
    dandelion tea 166
    dilutions 164
    drowning perennial weeds 163
    equipment 164–165
    grass clippings 166
    green leaves and shoots 163–164
    horsetail 166
    seaweed 167
post-hole composting 22, 75–76
potential problems
    ant infestation 113
    badgers 115–116
    bees and wasps 113
    flies 113
    grass snakes and slow worms
        114–115

herbicides 121
maggots 114
moisture levels 120
mould growth 121–122
odours 122
perennial weeds and seeds
    in compost bin 124–125
    drowning 123
    drying method 124
    light exclusion 124
with pH levels
    acidic compost 112–113
    alkaline compost 113
plastics and packaging 121
rats
    bin location 116–117
    human intervention 118
    leptospirosis 119
    material being composted
        117–118
    physical barriers 118
    vermin and wooden bins
        118–119
    temperature levels 119
    whitefly 114
    with worms 125–126

Rudolf Steiner's system of biodynamic
    agriculture 9

sheet composting 22, 74
soil carbon sequestration 12
submersion composting 35

trench composting 22, 75

vermicomposting 17, 132
vermiculture
    on commercial scale 132
    on home 133
    wormeries (see wormeries)

Weil's disease 119
wormeries 29
    bedding 140
    compostable materials 134
    contained wormeries 136–138
    dog and cat faeces 143–144
    feed 140–141
    garden wormeries
        dug-in worm beds 140
        raised worm beds 139
    indoor wormeries 138
    materials to avoid 135
    moisture 141
    pH level 141
    temperature 141–142
    ventilation 142
    worm bedding 135–136
    worm wee 143

First published in 2023 by
The Crowood Press Ltd
Ramsbury, Marlborough
Wiltshire SN8 2HR

enquiries@crowood.com
www.crowood.com

British Library Cataloguing-in-Publication Data
A catalogue record for this book is available from the British Library.

ISBN 978 0 7198 4285 6

Typeset by Simon and Sons
Cover design by Blue Sunflower Creative
Printed and bound in India by Thomson Press India Ltd.